Keeping the Brain in Mind: Practical Neuroscience for Coaches, Therapists and Hypnosis Practitioners

By Shawn Carson and Melissa Tiers

Forward By Lincoln Bickford

Changing Mind Publishing

New York, NY

2014 By Shawn Carson and Melissa Tiers

Keeping the Brain in Mind: Practical Neuroscience for Coaches, Therapists and Hypnosis Practitioners

Contents

Acknowledgements   5

Preface by Lincoln C. Bickford MD PhD   6

Introduction   9

Chapter 1: Hebb's Law, Long Term Potentiation
and the Quantum Zeno Effect   12

Chapter 2: Self-Directed Neuroplasticity   30

Chapter 3: Memory   56

Chapter 4: Implicit Memory and Priming   119

Chapter 5: Mirror Neurons   127

Chapter 6: The Eyes and the Visual Cortex   134

Chapter 7: Bad Dopamine   154

Chapter 8: The Emotional Brain   170

Chapter 9: Hemispheric Specialization   181

Chapter 10: Space and Movement   202

Chapter 11: Identity   229

Chapter 12: The ACC and Attachment Styles   236

Chapter 13: Libet and Unconscious Influence   244

Chapter 14: Conclusion   250

About the authors   253

Index

Acknowledgements:

The authors want to thank all the pioneers in cognitive neuroscience, Neuro linguistic programming, clinical hypnosis and social psychology. Their research and ongoing curiosity is contagious and we are happy to have been infected.

This book owes a massive debt to the work of Dr. Jeffrey Schwartz, who's four step protocol for self-directed neuroplasticity gave us the research and brain scans to validate our own work and that of our favorite teachers.

To our friend and teacher, John Overdurf, who's work and ideas continue to inspire us and all the people we teach, our gratitude is beyond words.

Foreword

Keeping the Brain in Mind is that rare gem of a book that seamlessly and accessibly delivers deep theoretical understanding with savvy practical guidance on how to apply it. And it does so with a spirit of curiosity and wonder towards this marvelous instrument, the brain-mind, through which we experience our world. It is a textbook, manual, and mental playground all in one. After many years studying the brain as a neuroscientist and learning to work with the mind as a psychiatrist and meditator, it is a refreshing surprise to read something that teaches me equally about both, and which brings new insights into their interplay. In particular, the authors present a series of intuitive and plausible models for how the brain and mind co-create one another, can be understood as metaphors for one another, and can be used to reshape one another bidirectionally in feedback loops for positive change.

But then, I've come to expect nothing less from Melissa Tiers and Shawn Carson, both consummate masters of metaphor, and master trainers of hypnosis, Neuro-Linguistic Programming, and coaching. I've studied with them in workshops and intensives over the past several years, and they consistently open my mind to new ways of helping clients re-frame problems into solutions and achieve growth. They are my go-to referrals for clients who are ready for change through hypnosis and coaching, and also for colleagues looking to expand their tool-kits. Both Shawn and Melissa are characterized by their voracious and broad curiosities as well as their can-do, flexible, determined-yet-relaxed stance when faced with challenging problems. In this book they range fluidly from the nitty-gritty of neural circuits underlying processes such as memory, attention, and emotion, to real-world clinical scenarios, to larger questions of identity, consciousness, and spirituality.

I'm not sure exactly where their 'inside scoop' is, but Shawn and Melissa have managed to identify most of the developments in neuroscience that I've found most interesting over the years -- such as neuroplasticity, memory reconsolidation, and mirror neurons -- plus a whole lot more. Either they don't sleep and spend nights poring over the neuroscience literature, or they have an uncanny radar for sorting the wheat from the chaff! They home in on those discoveries that can provide handles by which to understand the most efficient neural avenues to effect change and explain them in straightforward lay terms, they elucidate plausible mechanisms by which many 'old standard' NLP patterns -- including the coaching pattern, swish, and fast-phobia cure -- operate on the brain, and they suggest several new technical approaches. They then also flip these neural principles around, translating them into metaphors by which to help clients consolidate and make sense of their gains and inspire ongoing self-discovery. I would recommend this book even to expert scientists and therapists, expecting that it will reshape, rewire, reconsolidate, and re-enrich understandings and enthusiasm for our fascinating field; it certainly has for me!

Finally, it should be noted that Melissa and Shawn write in a playful and compelling style consistent with their coaching work, with layers of hypnotic language that serve to teach the material directly to the adaptive unconscious and allow new understandings to unfold long after the last page is turned. While reading the book, I regularly found myself going into trance and having "ah-ha" moments of novel connection and understanding, and you may, too. Likewise, since delving into this book, I've also found myself, while working with clients, utilizing new and unexpected ways to help people with the knowledge, metaphor, and techniques that wait to be discovered within...

Lincoln C. Bickford, MD, PhD
Psychiatrist, Columbia University Medical Center
Abbot and Director, SevenStars TaiChi TaoTemple

February 16th, 2014
New York, New York

Introduction

Imagine finding out that the work you have been doing in hypnosis, coaching, and therapy has been rewiring brains—literally. Keeping the brain in mind explores and outlines skills to help you do this more strategically. In the following chapters, you will learn how to target specific areas of the brain to reinforce new neural patterns while coaxing old ones into extinction. Once you learn the basics of brain science as it relates to learning, memory, fear, and habituated patterns, you will see how using this knowledge can dramatically improve the results of your sessions.

As coaches and trainers of practitioners of all kinds, we felt compelled to share how our work and the work of our students have been transformed by neuroscience. Watching our clients change how they think of themselves and their abilities made the decision to write this book, in which we share our strategies, an easy one. We know that once you get a glimpse of what is happening in the brain when you do your change work, your practice will never be the same again.

We are not neuroscientists. Not even close. We are just fascinated by the aspects of brain science that apply to our work. We work primarily with the unconscious mind—not with the outdated Freudian version, but with an understanding of the adaptive unconscious, which is as mysterious and multidimensional as the brain it works through. Even if you are not using hypnosis, neurolinguistic programming (NLP) or depth psychology, you too are working with strategies, programs, biases, and filters that are outside of conscious awareness.

This book will show you how to draw from and influence these programs in ways that make lasting changes in the brain. There is an old saying that "the mind takes the shape of what it rests upon." Now, science is proving this to be true, except it is the brain that takes the shape of what the mind focuses on.

We will teach you simple ways of bringing neuroscience to your clients so that they understand why and how they are changing. A little explanation goes a long way; so, we will share some of the most useful metaphors and analogies that inspire our clients to take control of their own brain.

This book will teach you different ways of calming the amygdala to break out of fears, phobias, and anxieties of all kinds. You will be able to arm your clients with practical techniques to stop panic in its tracks, rewire compulsive tendencies, and break habituated patterns and create healthy new ones. By understanding how to stimulate neuroplasticity more strategically, your clients will make changes faster, easier, and in a more generative way.

We focus a lot on memory because we believe it is the essence of change work. You will learn how to engage working memory in ways that stimulate long-term potentiation and disengage emotional reactivity. You will learn the different types of memory and how to work within them to create long-lasting changes.

Neuroscience provides a plausible mechanism for many, if not most, of the processes, techniques, and patterns that you use in your daily practice with clients. By understanding how these processes rely on the visual cortex, working memory, and reconsolidation, you can explain to your clients why techniques such as the "Swish," "Map Across," "Change Personal History," and re-imprinting work. We will show you how to use this explanation to reinforce and reframe your sessions to build expectation and resilience.

When we describe a process, such as the "Visual Squash," as a possible method to stimulate hemispheric balance, please understand that we are theorizing. We know, based on certain studies, which brain regions are being over activated in relation to habituated patterns, and, from other research, we know how to change those patterns. Because we know various research-based ways of calming the amygdala, we have created interventions that draw on this, but there has not been a lot of research on the neuroscience involved in NLP or hypnosis. We hope this will change, but we are not holding our breath. Instead, we are stimulating our brains with all the cool implications that the current thinking in neuroscience means for our work and us.

We hope that the information in this book will make neuroscience practical for you. We make every attempt to give you examples and demos of how to utilize each and every concept covered. There are countless books that dive deep into the brain. This is not one of them. We cover only those aspects that help people to change their minds, and in doing so, change their brains.

Chapter 1: Hebb's Law, LTP, and the Quantum Zeno Effect

Our clients come to see us with four types of problems. They feel something they don't want to feel, do something they don't want to do, don't do something they need to do, or they want to do something better. Their problem starts with a thought. Whether conscious or unconscious, these thoughts couldn't happen without a brain.

Your brain, protected inside a thick bony container called your skull, which is balanced rather precariously on top of your spine, is three pounds of matter representing the most complex, sophisticated, and confounding organ ever to be studied. Your brain contains 100 billion neurons, each of which is able to make contact with tens of thousands of others; the number of potential connections within your brain is in the hundreds of trillions. That's a number even the brain has a hard time imagining!

There are two things about the history of brain research that always amaze us. The first is that it has only been in the past 150 years that we have really known anything at all about this amazing organ. The second is how much has been learned in the past 30 years.

Of course, ancient man knew that he had a brain inside his skull, but the purpose of it was a mystery. The ancient Egyptians lovingly preserved the bodies and vital organs of their Pharaohs so that these nobles could enjoy a long and prosperous afterlife, but they thought so little of the brain that they extracted it rather unceremoniously from the skull using a hooked instrument that they poked into a body through the nostrils. After all, what use would a Pharaoh have for such a seemingly useless organ as a brain in the afterlife?

The Greek philosopher Aristotle (384-322 BCE) apparently believed that the brain acted as a radiator to cool the body. The Greek physician Galen (130-200 CE) was slightly better informed, believing that the brain was the organ of sensation and movement. It was not until the middle of the 19th century that scientists and physicians began to seriously and methodically study the function of different brain areas. Although brain research could be easily studied using animals, 19th century scientists had to rely on studying the behavior of victims of various non-fatal head injuries or diseases when studying the human brain.

The most famous example of the effect of brain injury is that of the unfortunate Phineas Gage (1823-1860). In 1848, Mr. Gage was using an iron rod to tamp down explosive powder. This resulted in the not entirely unforeseeable result of the iron rod piercing Mr. Gage's skull. The injury left Mr. Gage alive and seemingly well (other than being blind in one eye), but severe and unwelcome changes in his personality emerged. Mr. Gage was transformed from a model of moral fortitude into a most unpleasant individual who was given to drinking and brawling; thus, demonstrating that certain brain areas had certain functions and processes.

In the 1860's and 1870's, two scientists, Paul Broca (1824-1880) and Carl Wernicke, (1848-1905) found that damage to areas for the left frontal and temporal lobes could lead to an inability to speak or understand language. This research gave rise to the names of the areas of the brain responsible for speaking (Broca's area) and understanding speech (Wernicke's area).

During the first three quarters of the 20th century, human brain research was led by the surgeons who literally had access to living human brains, with the 1950's being a particularly fruitful decade. The neuropsychologist and brain surgeon Wilder Penfield (1891-1976) began to map the human brain using live human subjects who were undergoing brain surgery under local anesthesia. In 1954, Penfield created the famous motor and sensory homunculus, which is still used virtually unchanged to this day. We will meet Wilder Penfield again in the Chapter 3, which discusses memory, as well as the unfortunate Henry Malaison (1926-2008), through whose ordeal the function of the hippocampus was discovered.

Also in the 1950's, biologist Roger Sperry (1913-1994) began his famous split-brain experiments, which led to our understanding of hemispheric specialization and his winning the Nobel Prize. We will meet him again in Chapter 9, which addresses hemispheric specialization.

Since Phineas Gage's unfortunate accident, our knowledge of how the brain works has accelerated in leaps and bounds. With the advent of sophisticated scanning techniques toward the end of the 20th century, scientists have been able to study the activation of different brain areas in normal healthy human beings in real time as those people went about various mental and physical tasks.

When we talk about brain scans we will, for simplicity, often refer to functional magnetic resonance imaging—or fMRI— however, modern research often uses a combination of different scanning techniques, such as electroencephalography (EEG), positron emission tomography (PET), magneto encephalography (MEG), computed tomography (CT), and tensor imaging. Each of these techniques has different advantages in terms of being able to measure the timing and location of brain activity, brain structure, and so on, which is why researchers may combine two or more scanning techniques to produce an image that combines the best of each.

As a result of these advances, we are able to understand more of how the brain operates and how this impacts our behavior. Although these disciplines are in many ways still in their infancy, scientists have been able to construct a complete map of a mouse brain. A little cheesy perhaps, but with advances in brain scanning and rapidly increasing computer capacity, futurists such as Ray Kurzwell at Google are already talking about the possibility of downloading a person's individual brain scan into a computer within the next few decades. This will give a whole new meaning to the phrase "backing up your hard drive"!

One of the most fundamental learnings has been how individual neurons behave with each other. Your brain is constantly rewiring itself. Scientists once believed that you were born with a certain number of brain cells, after which it was all downhill, but now we realize that new brain cells are being created all the time in a process called neurogenesis. In fact, your brain is so eager to make new connections that, on average, one million neural connections are made for every second of your life. But how does your brain know what connections to make, and what is the process that allows this to happen? The answer is referred to as Hebb's Law.

Hebb's Law

Even if you don't know much about neuroscience, if you are in the mind-field, you've heard of Hebb's Law, although you most likely don't know it by that name. Donald Hebb (1904-1985) was a psychologist working in the area of neuropsychology; that is, the psychology of the brain. Hebb worked with Wilder Penfield, who we mentioned earlier and will again. Hebb was fascinated with how brain surgery in children, which involved removing portions of the brain, appeared to leave the child able to regain much or all of her mental abilities, while the same surgery in an adult might be very damaging. This led Hebb to conclude that a child's brain is more plastic and better able to rewire to compensate for a damaged area. Hebb studied the mechanism of this rewiring and came up with a theory known as Hebb's Law. He stated this theory in his 1949 book The Organization of Behavior: A Neuropsychological Theory:

"When an axon of cell A is near enough to excite cell B and repeatedly or persistently takes part in firing it, some growth process or metabolic change takes place in one or both cells such that A's efficiency, as one of the cells firing B, is increased."

Fortunately for us, someone was able to simplify that to: "Neurons that fire together, wire together."

This means that if your brain fires off two neurons—or two networks of neurons, at the same time—then, they will begin to become wired together. For example, think of the Nike logo, the big check-mark. Perhaps it makes you think of the phrase "Just do it." The two networks get to know each other. It's almost as if they are reaching out and shaking hands with each other.

Ivan Pavlov (1849-1936) understood this principle when he paired the ringing of a bell to the feeding of his dogs. At some stage, the ringing of the bell would make the dogs salivate whether or not they were being fed at that time. This is known as classical conditioning, meaning that the stimulus—the bell in this case—automatically produces the result (the salivation).

16

Ultimately, if stimulus-driven neurons fire together enough times, they will always fire together. They will become part of one network. If they shake hands enough times, they become such firm friends that they never let go. Here are some more examples of Hebb's Law in practice:

You meet a man called James. You see his face, and that picture is stored in a network of neurons in your visual cortex. You hear his voice, and that sound is stored in a separate set of neurons in your auditory cortex. You learn various autobiographical facts about him, which are stored elsewhere in your brain. All these networks become linked to form a larger network representing "James." When you think "James," you see his face, you hear his voice, it comes to mind that he lives in Brooklyn, and so on.

You are also friends with Janet, and you build a mental representation of her as well, also held in a network of neurons in your brain labeled "Janet." James and Janet meet, begin dating, and become inseparable. Whenever you see James, you see Janet. Whenever you meet with Janet, James is there. After a period of time, your brain will begin to think of James and Janet as one unit. You will be unable to think of one without the other. As a result your brain links the network of neurons representing James to the network of neurons representing Janet to create a combined network representing James-and-Janet.

From that rather romantic example, let us move on to a more insidious one. During show and tell at school, you become nervous. Your presentation in college makes you extremely nervous. You have to give a presentation at your first job and are nervous to the point of panic. At some point in this process, your brain begins to wire together "give-presentation" and "nervous," to create one mental circuit "give-presentation=nervous." So, this is Hebb's Law. We will be going over many different ways of using this principle in coaching.

How Does Hebb's Law Work? Long Term Potentiation

Hebb's Law is based on a process that takes place within the brain called long-term potentiation or LTP. LTP explains how two specific neurons begin to become wired together. Returning to our metaphor of neurons shaking hands, LTP explains what happens immediately after they shake hands for the first time.

When the first neuron fires, it releases neurotransmitters that travel over to the second neuron. This signal may cause the second neuron to fire as well, but the second neuron also reacts in another way. It begins to open up further neurotransmitter receptors that were previously hidden or closed. Therefore, after the first signal has been sent and received, the second neuron becomes more sensitive, almost as if it's expecting another handshake. So when neurons fire, they tend to make neighboring neurons not only fire but to want to fire.

Using Hebb's Law and the Principles of LTP: Anchoring

LTP and Hebb's Law are the underlying neural processes involved in setting and collapsing anchors. Anchoring is the NLP process that uses an external stimulus to recreate a certain emotional state. The stimulus is called the "anchor." A kinesthetic anchor might be a touch, an auditory anchor might be a sound or a word spoken with a certain tonality, and a visual anchor might be a gesture or facial expression. You can think of it as the NLP version of Pavlov's classical conditioning.

Whenever we teach NLP, the question is always asked, "How long does anchoring last?" Richard Bandler, the cofounder of NLP, has been known to answer this question by raising his

18

middle finger at the questioner, a well-known visual anchor! In fact, the question is an excellent one and goes to the very heart of LTP and Hebb's Law, because the anchor will last for hours or days if it is set using LTP but can last forever if is set using Hebb's Law. Remember, Hebb's Law is essentially the long-term version of LTP.

This has important consequences for setting anchors when doing change-work. Just because you have set an anchor and tested it, does not mean that it is installed forever. When setting an anchor, LTP will cause neighboring neurons to be more receptive in the short term, even if no long-term conditioning has taken place.

Intensity and repetition are the keys to conditioning the anchor so that it will last over a longer period. In general, the more intensely and the more times the anchor is conditioned, the stronger it will become until finally Hebb's Law kicks in, and the anchor becomes more permanent. Obviously, if you try to condition the anchor too many times, the client may simply get bored, and you could end up anchoring boredom!

A second important lesson for coaching is not to be too concerned if you are setting an anchor with the client and the emotional response appears to be only weak at first. Remember, LTP simply raises the potential for one neuron to fire in response to another, it does not guarantee it. However, the more times you fire the anchor, the more of the surrounding neurons and neural networks will be recruited.

Example:

The following example uses the principles of Hebb's Law and LTP during a process of collapsing anchors. The client feels nervous when she has to give a presentation at work, which she has to do on Tuesday afternoon for her boss.

Coach: I would like you to think about something that you are totally confident about, something that you know you do extremely well.

Client: I play tennis well.

Coach: Are you confident about that?

Client: Yes!

[Now the coach has a reference experience in which the client feels a sense of confidence and will associate the client into the experience of playing tennis and set an auditory and kinesthetic resource anchor. The anchor is set by touching the client on her shoulder, as well as using the words "you're feeling confident," in a specific confident tonality that matches the tonality used by the client. In NLP, this is called "stealing anchors."]

Coach: I would like you to think about the last time you played tennis.

Client: I played on the weekend, on Sunday.

Coach: So it's Sunday, and where are you? [Note the coach shifts into the present tense to begin to associate the client into the experience.]

Client: I am at the club, playing tennis with my regular partner.

Coach: What are you seeing? What are you hearing?

Client: I hear the sound of the ball on the racket and the sounds of the other matches around me.

Coach: And how are you feeling?

Client: I'm playing well and feeling confident.

Coach: You're playing well, and you're feeling confident. And when you're feeling confident, where do you feel that? [The coach begins to set the auditory resource anchor "feeling confident," and begins to build the state of confidence in the client.]

Client: I feel it in my chest! [The client begins to show responses associated with the state of confidence.

Coach: That's right; you're feeling confident in your chest. [The coach sets the kinesthetic anchor by touching the client on her shoulder. *Always ask permission before you touch the client.*] Now the anchors are set, and each time they are fired by touching the client's shoulder and saying, "You're feeling confident," the client's brain will begin to recruit neighboring networks of neurons, which will, in turn, build a bigger resource state. The coach begins to explore what these neighboring networks might be by asking questions about the state of confidence while the client is feeling confident.]

Coach: And as you're feeling confident in your chest, whereabouts in your chest is it when you're feeling confident?

[Notice that the coach continues to use the phrase "you're feeling confident" to fire the anchor and maintain the client's state of confidence.]

Client: It's in my heart!

Coach: So you're feeling confident, and it's in your heart, and when you're feeling confident in your heart, is there a size or shape to this confidence?

Client: It's like a golden glow!

[The principles of LTP suggests that these associations between the touch on the shoulder, the phrase "you're feeling confident," the picture of the golden glow in the client's chest, and the feeling of confidence may not yet be permanently wired together yet, but they are more likely to be triggered at the same time when one or more of them is triggered. The coach conditions the anchor further and tests the theory, first, by applying a break state, then by firing the anchors.]

Coach: Do you have plans for the weekend?

[This is a break state. We will talk more about break states and pattern interrupts later. But we digress . . . .]

Client: I'm going to a barbecue.

Coach: And you're feeling confident about that [Touches client's shoulder . . . Client shows responses of confidence. In this case, the coach is testing the anchor to make sure it elicits the state of confidence.] . . . Great, feel the golden glow in your heart! And as you are . . . feeling confident [touches shoulder] . . . see your boss's face as he listens to your presentation, and notice how it's different.

[The coach now begins to use the principles of LTP to anchor the state of confidence onto the boss's face. This time, it will not be sufficient to use a temporary anchor based on LTP. We want to permanently wire confidence onto the context of giving a presentation for the boss. This requires a lot more conditioning.]

Coach: That's right! As you're feeling confident [touches client's shoulder] and feeling that golden glow, see your boss's face as you give that presentation, and notice how it's different!

[The more times the coach repeats this pattern, the more LTP operates to wire confidence to the boss's face. Over time,

Hebb's Law kicks in to make the change permanent. We must also permanently wire the state of confidence onto other contexts in which the client may have to give a presentation to ensure that the confidence is generalized as far as possible. An example of this is not demonstrated here.]

So in summary:

- LTP links together neurons and neural networks, which fire at the same time.
- Leading your client to feel a state of confidence (or some other resource state) at the same time that you set a kinesthetic anchor (touch her) or an auditory anchor (saying a word or phrase with a certain tonality) uses LTP to link the anchor to the state.
- LTP can be used to make the anchor stronger through repetition.
- LTP can be used to make the state of confidence more powerful by bringing in neighboring neural networks. This can be done by asking the client for more details about the state, where she feels it, size, shape, color, etc.
- LTP can then be used to transfer the resource state of confidence to where the client needs the resource by firing off the anchors and then having the client imagine being in that context: "Feel confident and see your boss's face."
- Repeating the process a number of times and with enough intensity triggers Hebb's Law and permanently wires the resource onto the context where it is needed.

Quantum Zeno Effect

Do you ride the subway or the bus or walk in a busy city? Suppose you're standing next to someone and that person nudges you. Now you're watching out for that person. You're aware of the person, having, a temporary sensitivity, an awareness.

When you get off the subway, if you don't see that person for a month, you forget the encounter. You wouldn't recognize the person, but supposing the person had nudged you twice, or even three times, then you would really notice him or her. If the person even leans in your direction when seen again, you would react. This is what your neurons do. When two neurons fire at the same time, the wiring doesn't change, but the neurons do become more sensitive to each other from that very first time they fire, creating a temporary sensitivity that lasts perhaps a day or two, which is LTP. The more times the neurons fire, the more permanent LPT becomes, the less energy it takes to maintain LTP, and as LTP continues, it leads to a permanent rewiring, which is Hebb's Law.

Now, suppose Melissa was on the subway and a person nudged her and made a snide comment, which really pissed her off. She might walk away, but she would be replaying the encounter and thinking of all the different ways she could or should have responded. Suppose she then sees Shawn and tells him about the incident and gets all worked up again. Then, when she goes home at night and her daughter asks, "How did your day go?" She'll say, "It started off really messed up because of this guy on the subway . . . ."

Running these thoughts around like this is called the Quantum Zeno effect. It's different from LTP because, now, the effect doesn't have to be about the actual guy nudging you, it can be just remembering what happened, replaying it, thinking about it, imagining it, talking to yourself about it, or beating yourself up because you didn't say anything to the guy. All these reactions reinforce the neuronal link between the subway, the guy, and the negative emotion because just replaying incidents, good or bad, in the imagination also wires them together. What is fantastic for us, as change workers, is that it works the other way as well. Just imagining what you want to happen and how you want to be begins to wire you and circumstances in that direction.

The Quantum Zeno effect is a principle in quantum physics that states that observing the rate of decay of a particle or system actually slows down the decay. In other words, the process of observation stabilizes the system—a case of "a watched pot never boils." This isn't just a theory; it has been tested in the laboratory. Physicists have looked at anatomic particle and found that by observing it and checking on it, it becomes stabilized longer than an atomic particle that isn't being constantly observed.

The Quantum Zeno effect also applies to thought in general and neural networks in particular. The more we put our attention on something, the more it tends to persist.

When someone says, "Oh, I have this problem, and it's terrible, and it happens all the time," she is stabilizing the problem. If she wanted to get rid of the problem, all she would really have to do is stop thinking about it! This may sound ridiculous and way too easy, but if a person stopped thinking about a problem and started thinking about what she wanted instead, that problem would disappear by itself.

Let's be clear, though. When we say "problem," we mean something emotional or behavioral. Suppose you're scared of being bitten by your neighbor's dog. That might be an emotional issue for you if you were bitten when you were younger and now fear all dogs, but if you're scared of being bitten by your neighbor's dog because your neighbor's dog is crazy and tries to bite you all the time, that's a very different type of problem. For that, don't call us; call animal control.

Most problems we see are being stabilized through constant attention. Our clients ruminate in many different ways about how they feel and think about their problems, and they worry that they will never be able to change them. This is the Quantum Zeno effect as played out in countless therapy and coaching sessions across the globe. The important point is that research really does back up the idea that you get what you focus on. This fact gives you a great reason to interrupt your client's story by using a pattern interrupt to begin to break the Quantum Zeno effect.

Now there are many ways to do this, but if you can explain the reason for pattern interrupts to the client in a simple, concise way, then the client will begin to understand the process and won't think that you're just not listening or being rude or that you don't care. You're showing the client that the more you interrupt, the more you do care:

> "Here's why I'm not going to sit here and listen to the same story you've been telling your therapist for 30 years. Obviously, it hasn't helped you, has it? You've kept that story since you were 7 years old. And every time you tell it, you groove it a little deeper into your brain. My job is to teach you how to rewire it."

Clients' stories feel very present and real to them because they keep telling the stories, observing them, and stabilizing them in the brain. They're really solidifying the associated neural networks. One way change can happen naturally is that the person simply gets so bored of her own story that she no longer gets satisfaction from telling it. Everyone has heard it, and no one is interested, not even her. One typical way of getting fed up and bored with one's own story is to go see a therapist and talk about it for 30 years. This is why, sometimes, by the time we get the client, she is ready to change!

Another way a person can get rid of the satisfaction of telling the story is to not have an audience. Any performer knows that without an audience, there's no feedback and the show goes flat. So, as a practitioner, stop being the goddamn audience! If you listen to that old story, you're letting your clients reinforce their patterns because the more they tell the stories; the deeper they dig themselves into the hole about them.

Learning about the brain changes the whole dynamic of traditional psychotherapy. When the therapist asks questions like, "How does that make you feel? Why do you think you feel this way?" In using these statements, all the therapist is doing is solidifying that problem in the client's brain. So, the Quantum Zeno effect is a great metaphor to bring in as part of the big-picture metaphor of neuroplasticity that we discuss in the next chapter.

On the flip side, when we get the client into a positive state, and we ask questions such as . . .

> "How do you want to feel instead? And when you feel good that way, how do you know? What are you seeing when you feel this good? What are you hearing? Where do you feel that great feeling in your body? What is that feeling like? What are the size, the shape, and the color of the feeling? Why do you want this fantastic feeling to continue in your life?"

We create more links in the positive network. Remember, neurons like to make friends. Our brain is extremely social. The more connections we make in the different regions of the brain, the more opportunity we have to take it from working memory and LTP into a lasting, long-term association using Hebb's Law and into long-term memory.

So the next time you're with a client, don't spend your time listening to that old story. Ask the client what she wants and how she wants to be that's different from how she has been.

Ask her who she wants to be as a person and what it's like when she is that person.

The Brain's Tendency to Generalize

Because of LTP and Hebb's Law, the brain tends to generalize. It likes to link up situations and contexts that are actually different. This is how phobias develop. For example, they have a bad experience in one elevator and they generalize it to all elevators. If someone has been afraid in one elevator, how does that person know that she will be afraid in another one? The answer is generalization, and generalization is a byproduct of Hebb's Law.

The more links and associations the client has on a problem, the stronger it is. When a client has a fear of all elevators, that fear is much stronger than a fear of one particular elevator. Although this sounds like a silly thing to say, it is actually key to understanding the process of change work. Because when we really understand Hebb's Law and the process of generalization, then we can change our client one elevator at a time. We can use the process of generalization to turn a few small victories into a complete transformation.

The brain does not simply generalize according to context; it also generalizes according to emotional state because the brain will sort for like-minded states. State-dependent memory is the brain's tendency to make neuro-associations and link similar states together. You can think of states as being like colored threads in a tapestry that tells the story of the client's life. If you pull on the red thread that represents their fear, you can find all of the times in the past that the client felt that fear and all the times in the future when the client thinks she will feel it. One of the things that we do as change workers is to begin to weave new threads, better colors, into the tapestry of the client's life.

So when someone is depressed, she is in a certain biochemical, neurological, and energetic state, and everything she looks at gets colored by that state. From that depressed state, when the person thinks about her past, all that stands out are the depressing memories, and the person assumes that her future will be equally as bleak.

Until you dissociate a client from her negative neurophysiological state, you can't help her find solutions. This is why dissociation and pattern interrupts are crucial in change work. You've got to get the client out of the problem and into a more neutral emotional state before the resources need to find the solution are found.

This is why it is vital to be able to calibrate the client's state at any point in the session. You need to know what the clients look like when they're in the problem state, and you need to know what they look like when they're feeling resourceful so that you can move them between the two.

You need to have enough compassion to interrupt clients' old story and the patience to attach the resource they need to as many contexts—as many elevators—as necessary for the brain to begin to generalize the solution in the same way that it previously generalized the problem. Hebb's Law will do the rest.

Chapter 2: Self-Directed Neuroplasticity

So, now we know how individual neurons begin to wire up to each other under the principles of LTP and Hebb's Law. We've also had a glimpse inside a coaching session of how to utilize these principles to create new connections and responses. It's time for us to begin to examine the question, "Can I change my own brain by changing my mind?"

In this chapter we are going to talk about self-directed neuroplasticity, which is a fancy way of saying that by using your mind, you can actually change the physical structure of your own brain. Having read this far, this probably seems obvious to you, but for many years, most neuroscientists believed that the mind did not exist at all.

The mind was considered to be merely an "epiphenomenon" of the brain, a grand illusion created by the brain to make us think that we were more than just biological machines. This illusion, they believed, was caused by the firing of patterns of neurons in the brain, and neuroscientists referred to our experience of self as "Neural Correlates of Consciousness." Because the mind was an illusion, there was no way that the mind could have an impact on the physical structure of the brain. Others had a different view. For example, the Dalai

Lama, who has a fascination with neuroscience, had long believed that mind can change the brain. He had questioned neuroscientists on this possibility and was told that our mind arises out of our brain activity. The brain changes the mind, but the mind, it was believed, could not change the brain.

Now we know how wrong that belief was. Current research proves the mind can indeed alter the physical structure of the brain and can do so with every new experience a person has. This is called experience-dependent neuroplasticity. It's the brain's ability to change and the subject of a whole new wave of research and books.

The Dalai Lama, working with various neuroscientists, such as Richard Davidson, has begun to map out the neuroplastic effects of meditation on the brains of Buddhist monks. As you can guess, they have discovered that the monks are able to change the physical structure of their brains through traditional meditation practices; that is, through force of mind [Lutz A, et al. Long-term meditators self-induce high-amplitude gamma synchrony during mental practice. *Proceedings of the National Academy of Sciences U S A*. 2004;101(46):16369-73.]

A quote we love is "The scientists climbed the mountain and found the mystics sitting there waiting for them." On many levels, science is finally catching up with what many traditions have already known to be true. Dr. Jeffrey Schwartz, a psychiatrist at the University of California at Los Angeles (UCLA) School of Medicine, who we will be talking more about shortly, got his four steps to self-directed neuroplasticity from traditional Buddhism. Most great advances come from people who can step outside of the box, or from those who have no idea where the box even is.

It's important to understand why neuroplasticity is such a big deal. You see, before the discovery of neuroplasticity, it was thought that the only way a person could change her brain was through outside influences such as brain surgery or psychoactive pharmaceutical drugs. Experience-dependent neuroplasticity has proven that you can change your brain simply by using your mind in a different way, which opens up more possibilities than this book can cover.

One neuroscientist, Helen Mayberg, demonstrated that patients with depression showed the same changes in brain function using placebos as patients who received antidepressant drugs. [Mayberg HS, et al. The functional neuroanatomy of the placebo effect. *American Journal of Psychiatry*. 2002 .;159(5):728-37] We discussed the placebo effect elsewhere in the book, but the point is that if it was not the antidepressant drugs that were creating the changes in the brain, what was it? As it turns out, it was the mind. A more specific answer comes from other researchers, including Dr. Schwartz, who devised a simple protocol to assist patients with obsessive-compulsive (OCD) to change their minds, and from that, change their brains.

Dr. Schwartz's research allows us to reasonably argue that when we use hypnosis or an NLP technique that has the same underlying structure as his protocol, we too are creating changes in our clients' brains. We believe his four-step process provides a firm foundation for discussing neuroplasticity in the context of change work.

In his study on patients OCD, Dr. Schwartz divided the participants into two groups, one of patients who took psychoactive drugs (which were the control group) and one of patients who were taught a simple four-step mental protocol developed by Dr. Schwartz. The brains of both groups were scanned prior to the treatments, and then again after 10 to 12 weeks. What Dr. Schwartz and his research team found was that the same positive brain structure changes occurred in both the control group who took drugs and the study group who followed Dr. Schwartz's four-step protocol. By simply thinking about their OCD in a different way, the test group had physically changed the structure of their brains and did so without any of those nasty side effects of medication [Schwartz JM, et al. Systematic changes in cerebral glucose metabolic rate after successful behavior modification treatment of obsessive-compulsive disorder. *Archives of General Psychiatry.* 1996;53(2):109-13.]

Schwartz proved that thinking about problems in a different way leads the client beyond what the medical establishment considers "placebo" in that it made a real observable change in the physical structure of the brain. It created the same physical change as medication. Further, whereas when a patient stops taking drugs, the brain may revert to the old loop, the patients receiving change work therapy in Dr. Schwartz's protocol learned a skill, which makes change self-directed. The patient can continue to make positive changes in her life simply by using her own mind.

So, as the saying goes, the brain really does take the shape of what the mind rests upon. The Quantum Zeno effect, which we discussed in the previous chapter, says that it's what you continually focus on that changes the brain. In the case of Dr. Schwartz's protocol, it was focus on anything except the OCD that created the change. But the mechanism holds true in any other field. For example, if you play an instrument over and over, the areas of your brain responsible for playing that instrument actually increase in density; they get bigger and stronger. So, we are always changing the shape of our brain, for good or bad.

Keep in mind that as a hypnotist, coach, or change worker, you've been working with neuroplasticity all along, even if you weren't aware of it. Any time you learn something new or are using your conscious mind to change how you think, feel, or behave, you are changing the brain. As practitioners, that is essentially what we are teaching our clients to do.

Before we go on to describe Dr. Schwartz's four-step process in detail, we will consider the brain processes involved in OCD behaviors that underlie his protocol. The model that follows is based on the one laid out in Dr. Schwartz's seminal book You Are Not Your Brain. Note that the model is not intended to be complete and could be misleading for other types of problems, but it does represent a useful metaphor for describing how the brain works in the context of OCD.

As we know, the amygdala is a part of the brain that senses threats and creates a state of fear to protect us from danger. The last time something made you "jump out of your skin," you experienced the amygdala at work. The insula (insular cortex) is a portion of the cerebral cortex that has numerous functions, including the monitoring of internal states, such as our heartbeat; different emotional states; and "gut feelings." The last time you just had a certain sense or feeling that you couldn't trust someone, your insular cortex was doing its job.

The anterior cingulate cortex, a portion of the cortex, has a number of functions, one of which is error detection. You've surely experienced a situation in which you felt something was "not quite right." This was your anterior cingulate cortex doing its job.

These three brain areas, amygdala, insula, and anterior cingulate cortex are what Dr. Schwartz calls the "Uh-Oh Center" of the brain; the part of the brain that tells you something is seriously amiss. First, the anterior cingulate cortex identifies an "error," something going wrong, in the world around you. Your insula begins to notice that you're feeling a negative emotion, a gut feeling that something is wrong. Your anterior cingulate cortex and your insula begin to pass this feeling back and forth between them, making the negative feelings greater with each pass. At some point, your amygdala gets involved, and all hell breaks loose!

Next, let's visit the next brain area in Dr. Schwartz's model, the Habit Center, including the Reward Center:

The basal ganglia consist of certain parts of the brain that regulate behavior, especially behavior that is emotionally motivated. When you think about a habit that you have—perhaps biting your fingernails—your basal ganglia are involved. Part of the basal ganglia includes the accumbens, which is part of the brain's reward system. These areas are part of what Dr. Schwartz calls the Habit Center of the brain, the part of the brain responsible for engaging in automatic responses.

When the brain gets a message that something is wrong from the Uh-Oh Center, it looks for a way to avoid or otherwise find relief from the problem. This relief can be provided by the basal ganglia, including the caudate (automatic thoughts) or the putamen (automatic actions). When the basal ganglia have engaged in some automatic thoughts or behavior designed to provide relief, then the Reward Center (accumbens) is triggered and releases neurotransmitters such as dopamine, which creates good feelings in the mind and body. However, as we shall see, this relief is only temporary.

Let's move on to the final part of Dr. Schwartz's model, the Self-Referencing Center.

The frontal cortex, often called the executive brain, is involved in planning, organization, and error detection. When the reward center is triggered, the frontal cortex begins to learn that these habitual responses do indeed provide relief from the problem (even though the relief is only temporary), which further strengthens the feedback loop. Dr. Schwartz then moves on to discuss two areas within the frontal cortex, making up what he refers to as the Self Referencing Center. These are the medial prefrontal cortex (which we refer to throughout the book as the PFC), which is involved in working memory—including thinking about yourself—and the orbitofrontal cortex, which is also involved in decision-making and, when things go wrong, in obsessions.

These two brain areas, working together, can convince you that there is something wrong, and that something is you! Everything that you experience can seem to reinforce this message. This can lead to an even greater reaction from the Uh-Oh Center of the brain and further reinforcement of the compulsive cycle.

To summarize:

- Uncomfortable physical or emotional sensations are generated by the Uh-Oh Center leading to . . .
- Automatic responses by the Habit Center leading to . . .
- Release of neurotransmitters by the reward center leading to . . .
- Reinforcement of the circuit by the Self-Referencing Center of the frontal cortex.

But just when you may have concluded that the Blind Watch Maker who designed the human brain was either incompetent or sadistic, Dr. Schwartz finally discusses a brain area that can be helpful for dealing with OCD-type compulsions.

The Assessment Center

The Assessment Center is based on the lateral PFC, a part of the brain involved in voluntarily overriding automatic responses. By getting in touch with the Assessment Center, we can learn to override habits and compulsions, as we shall see.

Now on to Dr. Schwartz's Four-Step Process:

Dr. Schwartz calls the first step "relabeling."

In relabeling, patients are asked to identify the inappropriate thoughts and sensations that they have. This simply involves paying attention to them when they happen, making a mental note that they are happening, and labeling them. For example, "I'm experiencing my OCD thoughts again."

Dr. Schwartz calls the second step "reframing."

In reframing, patients are then asked to use the relabeling process to change the perceived importance of the thoughts and sensations they are experiencing; for example, by calling them "false brain messages": "Oh, I'm experiencing my OCD thoughts again, but that's not me that's just my brain."

Dr. Schwartz calls the third step "refocusing."

In refocusing, once the client has relabeled and reframed the OCD thought, she is told to redirect her attention to a more healthy activity or thought. This activity could be pretty much anything other than what that OCD is telling the client to do as long as it is healthy, useful, or productive. Some patients may choose gardening or exercise, others may choose listening to or playing music or deep breathing. The patient is to continue with the new activity for as long as possible or until the OCD thoughts go away.

When the patient voluntarily disregards the OCD thoughts in favor of the new activity, then she begins to strengthen her Assessment Center's ability to override the OCD. At the beginning of the program, the patient may only be able to carry out the new activity for a few minutes before the OCD becomes overwhelming and forces the patient to go back to the old routine, but over days and weeks, as the Assessment Center is strengthened, the patient will find it easier and easier to disregard the OCD messages.

Dr. Schwartz calls the fourth step "revaluing."

Finally, the patient is asked to reframe her experience by seeing the "false brain messages" and uncomfortable sensations created by OCD as being valueless, something to dismiss from the mind. Instead, the value of the alternate behavior is recognized: "That OCD was doing nothing for me, but look at how wonderful my garden looks now." (Assuming that the patient had redirected her activities towards gardening, of course!) In fact, any new activity, other than what the client has been doing, can break a pattern.

There was a nurse who worked in the psych ward. When patients came in and started to run their pattern, she would say, "Go and wash your hands." (Note: the patients did not have OCD!). Then, the nurse would tell them to sing two rounds of "Happy Birthday." If you think about that, it's action, it's moving forward, doing something, anything, different.

By the way, asking the patients to wash their hands and then sing "Happy Birthday," was also moving them between the two hemispheres of the brain, the left hemisphere then the right hemisphere. We will be talking a lot more about this in a later chapter.

How Do I Apply Dr. Schwartz's Protocol to Coaching?

Now, we are not suggesting that when your client has a compulsion or a craving you say to her, "Tell yourself, 'This is not me; it's just my brain,' and then go do some gardening." Instead, we have the client do something that immediately puts her into a much better state. In this sense, our techniques are much more sophisticated than Dr. Schwartz's four steps. The tools we have available as hypnotists and coaches go directly to the unconscious. We teach our clients techniques that are fast, empowering, and emotionally rewarding and give them a variety of ways to rewire the brain and coast through the four steps. They don't have to white knuckle it like they do in Dr. Schwartz's model because they learn how to stop the anxiety immediately and access the parasympathetic nervous system, which is the relaxation response.

These techniques also encourage flexibility in the brain by exercising the systems of attention and motivation while reducing emotional reactivity. Being able to navigate through emotional states has been proven to be the most important indicator of therapeutic success.

Understanding how to access the sympathetic and parasympathetic nervous systems is crucial in helping clients with affect regulation. The sympathetic nervous system is often described as the "fight or flight" response, and the parasympathetic nervous system is often described as the "rest and digest" system. Many of the clients we see—those with fears, anxieties or compulsive tendencies—could be described as having overactive sympathetic and underactive parasympathetic nervous systems.

Dr. Schwartz's model provides a valuable metaphor that explains to clients why they haven't been able to change and how things can be different now. We explain to clients that every time they do that habit, whether it's a craving, reaction, or a compulsion, they are reinforcing the neural network and going down the same old road or pathway. We explain that the easiest and most effective way to break habituated patterns in the brain is by interrupting them.

So we teach clients to think of the techniques taught them as roadblocks on the old neural pathway, leading them to take detours to new ways of thinking and feeling. Each time they interrupt the pattern, even after just three or four times, other areas of the brain are already starting to be engaged and making new connections. Neurons are making friends with other neurons.

Each detour means that the old path gets less use and, thus, weakens or gets overgrown while the new path gets cleared. Think of it like a forest. First, you have to cut through it to make a clearing for a path, and each time you walk across the new path, you widen it and so walking along it gets easier. Every time you start to feel a compulsion and immediately do bilateral stimulation or any other technique you will learn in this book, you will detour into the parasympathetic response. In traveling the new path, the old path becomes idle and starts to disappear as the old neural connections are pruned away.

When clients understand that they are not just stopping the feeling in the moment but are rewiring the pattern, it changes the whole game. They now have a reason to do the homework and acquire an understanding of how their minds can and do change their brains.

By explaining the basics of self-directed neuroplasticity to our clients, the problem becomes more approachable and the solution more accessible. Clients are given scientific reasons for why they haven't been able to change before and for how they can change now.

Labeling Thoughts and Emotions

Steps one and two of Dr. Schwartz's Four Step Process involve identifying and labeling "deceptive brain messages," including thoughts, physical and emotional sensations such as cravings, and habitual patterns of action or inaction. Dr. Schwartz describes a process of making mental notes of thoughts, emotions, and feelings as they arise: "I am thinking an angry thought." "I am experiencing a craving for doughnuts." Those readers interested in meditation and meditative practices will be familiar with the idea of labeling thoughts during meditation. The principles are the same.

There is some interesting research on the effects of labeling in this way. Matthew Lieberman and his team at UCLA used brain scanners while subjects labeled emotions with an appropriate word. When in an fMRI and shown scary faces, one group was told to label the images as: "That's anger" or, "That's fear." When they did, their brain activity moved from the amygdala (basic "fight or flight" response) to the more executive PFC (that is: "Let's think this through"). In contrast, the control group who saw the scary faces but didn't label them didn't experience reduced blood flow in the amygdala.

In effect, what Lieberman found was that subjects who put emotions into words, by labeling them, show greater activity in the Assessment Center and reduced activity in the Uh-Oh Center. Essentially, the process of labeling increased dissociation and decreased association with the emotions. [Lieberman MD, et al. Subjective responses to emotional stimuli during labeling, reappraisal, and distraction. *Emotion.* 2011; 11(3):468-80.]

Other research by James Gross of Stamford University in California also found that labeling emotions reduced their affect. Gross, however, also found that attempting to suppress emotions after they had been triggered increased activity in the Assessment Center (PFC) but did not result in reduced activity in the Uh-Oh Center (amygdala and insula). Gross concludes that trying to consciously control emotions (which he calls explicit control) is less effective at regulating emotional responses in the brain than unconscious emotional control (which he calls implicit control). [Gyurak A, et al. Explicit and implicit emotion regulation: a dual-process framework. *Cognition and Emotion.* 2011;25(3):400-12.] In fact, Gross concludes that the earlier in the emotional process that a change is made, the more successful regulation of that emotion is.

Application to Coaching

So the next time you are in a situation that might normally make you feel unresourceful, try labeling the emotion: "I am feeling angry." Notice what happens. When you begin to feel the anger or other negative emotion subside, you can label that as well: "I was feeling angry; now I'm not." This will give you the space to decide how you want to feel instead: "I was feeling angry; now I'm not, and I wish to feel peaceful instead." Just notice what happens.

Top-Down Processing

The thing that makes your human brain special is your PFC. The PFC is sometimes called the executive brain because it is responsible for planning our actions, like the CEO of a company. It is also responsible for complex social functions. Remember the unfortunate Phineas Gage who had an iron spike blown through his prefrontal cortex and became socially nonfunctional as a result? The CEO retired, permanently.

When the PFC is in charge, things are generally okey-dokey, not terrible, although not necessarily great. When information starts here, it is called "top-down processing," meaning your executive brain is running the show. Then there's the rest of your brain, the mammalian and the reptile brain. This is the part of the brain that knows what it's like to be eaten by something, so it easily overreacts. When that part is in charge, it's called "bottom-up processing," meaning that you are responding to some external stimulus, putting you in survival mode. Labeling forces you into top-down processing.

When God wanted Adam to be his right-hand man, he asked him to name everything in the Garden of Eden. There's this idea that if you label something, you can control it or explain it. It becomes a smaller bite. Instead of an overwhelming feeling, we have to step out of it to label and identify it.

Once we've defined a negative feeling, there's suddenly all this area that's not it. Then, it becomes a matter of where we choose to put our attention. Until we step out of the negative state, it's hard to choose a different one. The brain sorts and filters by emotional and biochemical state. Remember state-dependent learning. When you're sitting in a certain biochemical wash, everything you think of—your past, your present, and your future—is colored by that state. Until you can step out of it, you're going to have a hard time finding alternatives. This is why labeling is good. It dissociates.

But labeling a problem doesn't create a change by itself. We all have clients who walk in and say, "I have such and such disorder." They know exactly what they have. So, while labeling their problem may dissociate them a little bit, it also tends to give them something to identify with and, unfortunately, keep them growing into the diagnosis. The diagnosis itself acts as an attractor to which other symptoms are drawn. So you need the other steps to change the label and change the negative behaviors and feelings.

Gratification Delayed

When experiencing a thought or emotion in the moment and wishing to do something to relieve that feeling, Dr. Schwartz suggests asking the question "Why am I about to do this?" to help identify deceptive brain messages. In addition, he suggests a "15 minute rule," the rule being that you will wait for 15 minutes, and then make a decision about whether you really want to do it.

This is also based on well-researched phenomena in neuroscience that suggests that a temptation deferred is a temptation reduced. The longer we perceive we have to wait for the payoff for some activity, the less attractive the activity becomes. Even pushing the activity out for 15 minutes can make it much less attractive and, therefore, less compulsive [Kim B et al. Perception of anticipatory time in temporal discounting *Journal of Neuroscience, Psychology, and Economics.*2009;2(2):91-101.]

The HNLP Meta-Pattern

Dr. Schwartz's Four Step Process has now been explained in detail. We also have said that, as hypnotists and NLPers, we have sophisticated techniques that can be used in place of Dr. Schwartz's Step 3, "Do something different," that can produce even better results. Dr. Schwartz's studies validate the four steps we've been teaching our students and clients for many years. We call it the "meta-pattern" because it is the basis for almost every successful change process we can think of. If you take some time to think about all the patterns or successful interventions you use, we guarantee that you'll find it.

The Four Steps of the Meta-Pattern

Don't worry if you are unfamiliar with the meta-pattern; we will go through a lot of examples of it in this book. Each pattern that we run will follow the same sequence of four steps:

Step 1: Associate into the problem. We are going to have the client re-experience the problem just enough to light up the relevant circuits of the client's brain.

Step 2: Dissociate from the problem. By dissociating the client from the problem we turn off the problem circuits long enough to find a resource.

Step 3: Associate into a resource. Having turned off the problem circuits of the brain, we will now find a resource for the client and light up these resourceful circuits in the brain.

Step 4: Collapse the resource and the problem. We will begin to link the resourceful brain circuits with the problem brain circuits to create a new, integrated circuit. We will test and make sure that this new circuit is working appropriately in the context of the problem.

Let's go through to the steps and compare them to Dr. Schwartz's protocol.

Step 1

The first step of the meta-pattern is to associate into the problem, meaning to feel it, and be aware that you're feeling it. The reason this is so important in change work is that we have to first light up the neural networks representing the problem. If we don't do this, then we can make the client feel as wonderful and resourceful as we want in our offices, but those resources will not become attached to the part of the brain representing the problem, and will not be available when the client needs them in the real world. So, the first step of the meta-pattern is exactly the same as the first step of Dr. Schwartz's protocol, Relabeling.

Step 2

The second step of the meta-pattern is to dissociate. The reason why we need to dissociate the client from the problem is that the brain areas responsible for the problem are, by definition, not wired up to the appropriate resource. If the problem were wired up to the appropriate resource in the client's brain, then the problem would no longer be a problem! Therefore, as long as the client is in the problem state, it is going to be much more difficult for her to find a good resource.

Now, what happens when we label a feeling? We dissociate from it! We saw this when we discussed the work of Matthew Lieberman and James Gross. These researchers showed that activating the Assessment Center before the emotional response took hold (or, in this case, after the emotional response had died away) reduced activity in the Uh-Oh Center, the amygdala and insula. In Dr. Schwartz's work, the labeling takes the form of "It's just the OCD. It's not me; it's just my brain."

Step 3

The third step of the meta-pattern is to associate into the resource. What's a resource? A resource in the context of a problem is "anything that's not the problem." Why is this? It is because any mental activity that is not currently wired into the circuits representing the problem is new information for the brain. The problem becomes changed because the brain is rewired.

In theory, we can rewire any new information into the problem and, thereby, change it. Obviously, we will usually choose to wire-information loaded with positive emotional energy to counteract the negative energy of the problem. As we have discussed, Dr. Schwartz suggests that his patients choose to do something different that's healthy: go for a walk or listen to music—anything else will work.

Step 4

The fourth step of the meta-pattern is the collapse. From the resource, which is doing something else or feeling a better emotional state, we look at that problem and notice how it's different. We step out of the biochemical state of the problem, and the neural network representing the problem, so that we can choose a better perspective. Then, we look back at the problem from that more positive emotional place. As a result, the problem is trance-formed.

Dr. Schwartz tells his clients to reevaluate the old behavior from a more resourceful place. This reevaluation represents a collapse of the new state and the old state so that they become part of the same neurological network. When they do, the old neural network is transformed.

Now, if you have a background in NLP, especially Humanistic Neuro Linguistic Programming, or HNLP, developed by John Overdurf and Julie Silverthorn then you may be sitting there thinking, "So what? We've known the meta-pattern for years. Why is this a big deal?" Well, it's a big deal because now you can see the change in the neural networks on an fMRI. In our work, we help clients make rapid and powerful changes, but the medical establishment says, "Well, how do we know that's not just the placebo effect?" Obviously, we think the placebo effect is a good thing, but the pharmaceutical companies don't. They have to test all new drugs against a placebo, and no matter how good the results are, if the drug doesn't beat the placebo, pharma companies can't sell it. Unfortunately, they can't sell the placebo either! But now through Dr. Schwartz's research, we can see that running patterns, such as his Four Step Protocol (an example of the meta-pattern of HNLP), have the same physical impact on the brain as drugs, and, therefore, they are more than simply placebos.

In practice, the meta-pattern, in the office setting, works by simulation. There are many studies about how the brain reads and responds to certain words that create different sense impressions and emotions [Havas DA, et al. Emotion simulation during language comprehension. *Psychonomic Bulletin & Review*. 2007;14(3):436-41] and different actions [van Elk M, et al. The functional role of motor activation in language processing: motor cortical oscillations support lexical-semantic retrieval.
Neuroimage. 2010;50(2):665-77.]

If you read emotional words, your brain activity flows towards the emotional centers as well as the areas for processing language. If you read an action word—a compelling story about running, like a chase scene—at some point, your brain is going to start the "running" program in your brain. This means that we don't have to physically do an activity to stimulate the neural network involved. That allows us to rewire the circuits through imagination and rehearsal. When the brains of athletes who are visualizing sports practice are scanned, the same areas in the brain used when the sport is physically practiced light up, and the visualization training allows the athletes to outperform, in a very significant way, those athletes who only do physical training.

The HNLP Meta-Pattern in Practice

Let's consider how we can use the meta-pattern in practice to create change in the client:

Step one: Associate the client into the problem state by asking her to imagine that she is in a situation in which her problem normally arises. This allows us to gather a lot of information about the problem's trigger, including what the client is focusing on and saying to herself, how her body feels, what actions she is taking in response, and so on.

To re-associate the client into the problem, switch into present progressive tense language. That is, switch from "When was the last time and place this happened?" to "Where are you? What are you seeing, hearing and feeling?" This switch into the present tense will allow the client to feel the emotions associated with the problem. One study showed that using progressive tense verbs increases the emotional experience of memories [Hart W. Unlocking past emotion: verb use affects mood and happiness. *Psychological Science*. 2013;24(1):19-26.] By lighting up the emotional feelings associated with the problem, we are lighting up the "problem" networks in the client's brain.

Step two: Dissociate the client from the negative emotion by getting her to think of something else (a break-state or pattern interrupt). Alternatively, ask her to reevaluate the problem using her Assessment Center (i.e., labeling). One way to do this is to ask them to rate the problem on a scale of 1 to 10 (the Subjective Units of Distress Scale, or SUDS). Either way, dissociating the client gives her a more neutral position so we can help her to find a better emotional state.

Step three: Associate into that resource state, typically by asking the client what it like to actually feel resourceful. We want to get the client to fully embody a better, more positive, emotional state. Again, we will switch into present progressive tense to maximize these feelings: "What's it like when you're feeling confident!"

Step four: Collapse the two states by having the client think of the trigger while in the resourceful emotional state. This will neutralize the trigger, when conditioned-in through repetition. In neurological terms, we are wiring the brain circuits that represent the resource into the brain circuits that represent the context in which the problem previously arose.

So we have the four steps of the meta-pattern: associate to the problem, dissociate, associate into a resource, and collapse the resources to the problem. We haven't told you how to do it yet. The application of the meta-pattern that we use most often—in fact, the one that we use with almost all clients in every session—is the coaching pattern. This was taught to us by John Overdurf and is a conversational version of the meta-pattern.

The Coaching Pattern

The coaching pattern has the same four steps as the meta-pattern, in the following form:

Step one: Associate into the problem by asking, "Tell me about the last time and place this happened . . .." Then switching into

49

present-tense language to revivify the experience: "Where are you, what are you seeing, what are you hearing, what are you feeling?"

Step two: Dissociate from the problem by asking, "That's how you've been. How do you want to be different?" This invites the client to look at the situation from a dissociated viewpoint. It also uses past tense "That's how you've been" to shift the problem into the past.

In addition, we will use gestures to reinforce the unconscious instruction to change. When Melissa, for example, says, "That's how you been," She will typically use the right hand to "push" the problem into the client's past. When she says, "How do you want to be different?" not only is she embedding the command "you want to be different" in the client she is also typically using her left hand to gesture up into the client's right visual field, inviting her to visually construct the desired self.

Step three: Once the client has decided how she "wants to be different," invite the client to associate into that resource by asking, "What's it like when you are feeling that? Where in your body is that good feeling?" At the same time, use the left hand to gently "push" that new feeling inside her.

Step four: Once we see the client's physiology respond to the resource state—perhaps sit up straighter, have more body symmetry, and generally look more "resourceful"—we trigger the collapse by saying, "As you're feeling that now, look at that old issue and notice how it's different."

Of course, simply doing this once is not sufficient to change an issue that the client may have had for a long time. We have to run the pattern a number of times in a number of different contexts in order for it to generalize through the client's experience.

Here's an example:

Client: Every time I talk to my boss, I get anxious and feel like I'm going to panic.

Coach: When was the last time, specifically, that this happened? [Step 1 of coaching pattern]

Client: Just yesterday! He came into my office, and he had that look . . .

Coach: Stop! [The coach uses a pattern interrupt because she can see from the client's physiology that the she has already associated into the problem. If the client had not immediately associated into the problem, the coach would have continued gently probing the client with the present progressive tense, "Where are you? What are you seeing? What are you hearing?"]

Coach: How do you wish you could feel? When you talk to him, if you could feel any way, what would it be? [Step 2 of the coaching pattern.]

Client: Confident. I've been working there for 12 years. But he's the new boss, and he hates me. He feels threatened or something . . . [Although the client has identified a resource: "confident," she has returned to the problem state as indicated by her physiology as well as her comments. Because the client is in the problem state, we are still on step one of the process. The coach should not seek to help the client find a resource until she has dissociated from the problem.]

Coach: Threatened? Why do you think that is? [The coach seeks further information.]

Client: Because I know all the clients and how things should be, and everybody is used to me kind of being in charge.

Coach: Well, I suppose if I became the boss and found out someone was already doing my job and doing it much better than I could, I suppose I might feel threatened too . . . [The coach reframes the boss's behavior as "normal," and also seeks to change the state of the client by suggesting that she is more competent than her new boss. The coach is seeking to reframe the "meaning" of the boss's behavior from "he hates me" to "he is threatened." Doing so will allow the client to change states from "anxious" to "feeling sorry for" . . . See the discussion on semantic memory in Chapter 3 for more on reframing.]

Client: But he's such an asshole! If he would just ask me for help, I would gladly do it, but he disses me in front of everyone. [The client remains in the problem state. As long as she stays there she will find it difficult to find a good resource. The coach must dissociate her!]

Coach: Okay. So, you know you can run the place, right? And you're pretty confident that you know what the clients want, right? [The coach directly challenges the client; if the boss feels threatened it must be because the client is competent and dealing with the customers, and, if so, she must also be confident in her competence! Dealing with customers will provide a context in which the client already feels confident.]

Client: Yes. But he . . . [The client attempts to return to her old story, but the coach uses another pattern interrupt . . .]

Coach: And what's it like when you're feeling confident? Where in your body do you feel it? I mean, you've been doing this for over a decade, right? [The coach uses another pattern interrupt to break the client's pattern and dissociate her from the problem. The coach then invites the client into the resource state. This time the client begins to associate into a resource . . .]

Client: Yes. I feel my chest expanding when I'm confident, and things just flow easily . . .

[The coach is now able to collapse the resource into the problem . . .]

Coach: And as you're feeling that expanding and things flowing easily, knowing what you know, see your boss's face. How do you feel now?

Client: Well, a little better, but . . . [This was only the first iteration of the collapse. The process needs to be repeated several times to get the neural network associated with "confidence" wired into the network associated with the problem. Therefore, the coach repeats the process by associating the client back into the resource of "confidence."]

Coach: Now let's slip into that confidence again. Remind me what it's like when you're feeling it now? You'll find it easier if you sit up a bit straighter. Where does confidence move in your body?

Client: In my chest and then my shoulders, and I get this easy feeling in my core . . . [The client re-associates in confidence, so the coach does the collapse again . . .]

Coach: And as you're feeling this now, see that boss's face. How do you feel now?

Client: Better . . . he doesn't seem so threatening . . .

Coach: And as you feel more confident in that you can change and you sit up straighter and feel the flow, now see his face.

Client: Yes, much better. He seems smaller somehow . . .

[After the third iteration of the collapse, there is a submodality shift; the boss appears "smaller." See the Chapter 6 the visual cortex and submodalities.]

Coach: That's right. He has a lot of catching up to do . . . and as you feel the truth in that, now see his face.

Client: I kind of feel sorry for him. It must suck to be the boss, and no one respects you . . .

The coaching pattern has served to reframe the client's experience of her boss.

This is the pattern we use all the time. Step one gave us the info we needed; the trigger was the boss's face. Step two was to dissociate by asking the client what she wanted to feel instead of fear. We also encouraged dissociation by getting the client to talking about how long she worked at her job and how she felt she knew more than the boss did to reframe and change the semantic meaning of her experience. This led us easily into step three, which was to associate into confidence. By asking the client how her experiences felt in her body and by reminding her of how much she knew, we got her into a confident state through which to see her boss. Then, we repeated step three and four until we changed the response.

These four steps are underneath most of the processes and patterns that we use. They are also what make Dr. Schwartz's work successful.

We also arm our clients with different techniques so that they can immediately step out of the negative and into a positive state whenever they need to. Some of these techniques that will be covered in this book are:

- Bilateral stimulation
- Meridian tapping
- Peripheral vision

- Backward spin
- Heart-coherence breathing

Teaching techniques such as these to your clients will allow them to truly discover self-directed neuroplasticity for themselves.

Chapter 3: Memory

This chapter is about memory. Because change work is about learning, and learning is all about memory, this is the longest chapter in this book. Most of our job is to help our clients unlearn old habituated patterns and learn new ones instead. Understanding how different memories are stored and how to work within them is crucial for lasting change.

Neuroscience identifies five different types of memory: working memory, representing short-term storage of information; episodic memory, or memories of events; semantic memory, or memory of facts; procedural memory, meaning remembering how to do things such as riding a bicycle; and implicit, or hidden, memory.

Much of what we are doing in change work involves working memory. Working memory is a portion of the brain that is dedicated to maintaining attention on a specific task. Three areas of the working memory have been identified:

- A central planning area for keeping an overall plan in mind.
- A short-term visual memory that is able of playing a

short "video" loop.
- A short-term auditory memory that is able to play a short loop of sound or internal dialogue.

A good metaphor for thinking about working memory is a director, cameraman, and sound engineer at work. The director has an idea about what he is trying to achieve in creating a scene, the cameraman films a short video loop, and the sound engineer adds the soundtrack.

Timing plays an important part in working memory. The visual and auditory loops of the working memory are of a short duration. Some researchers estimate that the loops are as short as three seconds. The contents of all of the working memory begin to decay over time, with an estimated 30 seconds during which they can be recreated. You can think of this as the cameraman and audio engineer having only three seconds worth of film and the film being automatically deleted after 30 seconds or less. Sounds crazy, right?

Because the duration of the movie is short and fades quickly and the fact that people generally pay little attention to our internal processes, many do not even realize that they are playing these short-term memory "movies" in their heads. They may be watching depressing movies and feeling bad or watching horror movies and feeling fear without any awareness that they are doing so.

Learning and the Reward Circuit

The brain learns to stay away from danger while seeking rewards. It learns best when experiencing either a strong negative response, such as fear, or something very pleasurable, such as food or sex. When we get something good, such as food, our brain rewards us by releasing chemicals such as dopamine. Dopamine is released, alerting the hippocampus that something worth learning is happening.

The hippocampus responds by taking the experience that resulted in a reward—whether in the external environment or the contents of working memory—and encoding it into long-term memory. We're going to be talking more about the downside of dopamine and how dopamine tends to set your problems in place later on, but, for the moment, we are going to focus on another function of dopamine, learning.

To consciously learn, we have to pay attention. For example, if you have a client who's checking her texts in the middle of the session, she's wasting your time and her money because she's not paying attention. Her brain isn't taking in information in a way that will be easily accessed later. You see, there is a gate that stands between what a person is paying attention to and the rest of the world, with all its competing distractions, including text messages. If the gate is not closed, the client can't pay attention long enough to learn something new.

Dopamine closes that gate. Imagine a cave woman in the forest who finds a strawberry patch. The dopamine kicks in: "Oh, strawberries! Awesome." She pays attention to where the strawberries are, learning how to find them again for the future. That's the purpose of dopamine in locking-in the attention.

Without dopamine, you can still focus if you force yourself to in the way you focus on tasks that are mundane and boring. Dealing with paperwork and taxes come to mind. It's not a lot of fun to do boring tasks, like taxes, so, it is easy to be distracted by texts, emails, or just random thoughts while doing them. This is why a person may file her taxes on the last possible day! But a dopamine rush makes accomplishing things easy. You become so engrossed that you end up saying, "Wow, I've been doing this for X amount of hours? Where did the time go?" That's dopamine.

So we want you to have a lot of dopamine while reading this book!

And you want your clients to get the dopamine flowing during your sessions with them. Make your change work fun and engaging. Talking about how the brain gets rewired and how this rewiring is going make it easier to change captures the client's attention.

Once we have the client's attention locked in with dopamine, we have to decide what to do with it, but what do we mean by "attention"? As we have said, there's the director, the cameraman, and the sound engineer. So, you have your video, your audio, and the director making the movie, and the movie creates feelings in the body, but the feelings are not in working memory. You can think of your body and your feelings as the audience watching the movie and laughing and crying, depending on what the director is filming. Those feelings are felt whether or not a person is aware that the movie is playing. This is why people who do not track their internal movies can feel bad without knowing why.

If you want to experience your own working memory, think about something pleasant, such as an activity. Visualize it and hear the soundtrack. What would the title of the movie be if there was one? What did you learn from the movie? What was the big-picture message? And the more you enjoy the movie, the more dopamine you will generate!

If you can get dopamine flowing in the brains of your clients, and if you can lead them to have good video, audio, and a great title in their working memories, you can do change work. In fact, this is the basis of change work.

Using the Working Memory in Coaching

To optimize the client's ability to learn a new behavior or feeling in a particular context, make sure that the new behavior is being fully rehearsed in the client's working memory. The aim is to help the client create an overall plan of how this new behavior will fit into her life by having her see what she would see and hear what she would hear if the new behavior were being played out in real life. In addition, make sure that the new behavior being rehearsed has strong emotional content to provide the emotional energy needed to set it in long-term memory. Here is a short example:

Coach: How do you want to behave when you are giving the presentation?

Client: I want to be confident.

[The coach now begins to stimulate the planning area within the working memory.]

Coach: What will being confident do for you when you are giving presentations?

Client: I will be much more comfortable, and my career will be more successful.

Coach: So, when you're feeling more confident when giving presentations, you also feel comfortable, and this will result in you being more successful in your career?

Client: Yes!

Coach: And as you're watching yourself give this presentation while being confident, what do you see? [The coach begins to ask the client for the visual loop of the working memory.]

Client: I was seeing myself in front of the group, standing straight, looking everyone in the eye, and breathing easily. [The client provides a short visual loop. Note that this visual loop is currently dissociated; that is, the client sees herself in the picture.]

Coach: You would see yourself in front of the group, standing straight, looking everyone in the eye, and breathing easily. And what would you be hearing? [The coach respects the visual loop provided by the client. She also respects the short life of this loop, which will decay in 30 seconds, and, therefore, she repeats the contents of the visual loop to remind the client. The coach now asks the client to fill in the auditory loop by asking for sounds associated with the movie she is playing in her mind.]

Client: I would be hearing my own voice sounding confident and questions from the audience. There would be a tone of curiosity in the questions.

Coach: So you're seeing yourself in front of the group, standing straight, looking everyone in the eye, breathing easily, hearing your own voice sounding confident, and hearing questions from the audience with a tone of curiosity. [The coach continues to repeat the contents of the visual and auditory to remind the client. The coach now moves into the area of feeling to provide the emotional fuel to turn this into a long-term memory.]

Coach: Float into the you in the picture and see out of your own eyes . . . . How are you feeling? [The coach begins to hook the movie that the client is playing in working memory into the emotions felt in the body.]

Client: I feel good. Confident but relaxed.

Coach: That's right. Confident and relaxed. And the important thing about rehearsing this again and again is that research is proving that you are changing your brain as you do this. The brain learns how to respond even from imagination. Isn't that cool?

Client: Yes! So each time I imagine being confident in front of that group, my brain is learning to be that way? That is really cool. No wonder I was anxious before. I was rehearsing being nervous . . . .

Coach: You had been doing that. And now you're learning how to be confident, relaxed, and even curious as you imagine now, standing in front of that group . . . [The coach uses temporal language to remind the client that the problem behavior was what she *used to* do, and the coach loops the client through another rehearsal of the new feeling.]

Client: Yes. That feels so much better.

In our work, we are always bringing in little snippets of research to educate and motivate the client. A little dose of neuroscience goes a long way to help people change. For the most part, we are changing beliefs, and we, as a society, are used to changing our opinion based on the latest science news. In our culture, the gods of change are really the "Latest research," "Scientists say . . . " or, "What they're finding is . . . " and this has a way of engaging attention and shifting beliefs faster than anything else.

Putting the weight of science behind change work convinces the client that change is not only possible, it's inevitable. When we explain how the few moments the client spent in trance is now going to be laid down into the brain's long-term memory and how the unconscious mind works when the movie title of the client's issue is changed, then we're opening up the possibility for the client that, yes; change can be this easy.

To make any change permanent, the pattern must be repeated a number of times. That's why a change work session is an hour, not 2 minutes. To do a "collapse" of the problem may only take a few seconds, but the conditioning through repetition is going to turn a new behavior from merely long-term potentiation to neurons permanently wiring together.

Working memory has its own set of limitations and problems. If we are not aware of them, these limitations and problems can make learning new feelings and behaviors difficult for clients during change work. These problems are complicated by the fact that the content of the working memory fades quickly, perhaps prior to learning taking place. The coach can never underestimate a client's ability to get lost in the process!

The client could also use her working memory to counter the process during the session. For example, if we are doing a visual pattern with a client while her auditory loop is telling her, "This won't work," then there is a very good chance that the visual pattern won't work! Similarly, if we are using a verbal pattern, such as a reframe, while the client is making negative pictures in working memory, there is a serious risk that the reframe will not stick.

If a client comes in to see you, chances are that she is playing some messed up movies in her head. Remember, your job is to get her to play a good movie with a good sound track for a positive purpose and to encourage dopamine activation long enough to learn that.

The brain has purpose. The brain is directing the organism to survive, to stay away from the raptors, and to move toward food and sex. That's what the brain is doing; seeking to avoid pain and go toward pleasure. Everything we do in the modern world is just many different variations of this. Shopping, for example, is just one modern version of the caveman's going to the forest to find strawberries.

Remember, the purpose of a motive is essentially going to be reflected in what a person is saying to herself while running a movie in her mind. Think about a negative movie that you've run in your head recently, such as: "I can't believe he did that.

He's such an asshole." The purpose of the thought is to make sure you know that "he's an asshole," so you don't get fooled again. You'll replay what "he did" again and again because your brain wants you to remember to avoid him.

The purpose of the thought can be unconscious, and very often it is. Lots of people have very little awareness of what is going on inside their own heads, but if you listen to how they speak, you'll hear the purpose. Some people don't even know that they're running a movie in their heads. They think that they just "have" this problem or that a feeling just comes over them. They have no awareness that they are generating these feelings, which means they can learn to generate different feelings.

When your clients come in with issues, the purpose is to find the solution. So, what they want—the solution—is going to be the purpose of the video and audio of the new movie that you will be helping them create inside their heads. Of course, you've got to get the dopamine hit going. The new movie has to be captivating enough to hold attention and excite a client's reward circuits. In this way, every time a client plays the movie, the neural network is reinforced and the new way of thinking and behaving is locked in place. The stronger the dopamine hit, the more motivation to move towards the content of the movie. This is why addicts have very narrow and intense focus. If we could take the amount of energy, motivation, and focus that an alcoholic has to get alcohol, or that a drug addict has to get drugs, we could redirect massive amounts of energy towards a positive purpose.

Now, we are going to cover many different ways to change all three aspects of the movie inside clients' heads so that your sessions can be fun, engaging, and dopamine laced. Because the working memory is how we set and achieve long- and short-term goals as well as work with and reframe memory, a lot more time will be spent on learning how to work within it.

Episodic Memory

Episodic memory is the memory of past events and is most often related, at least consciously, to a client's problem. If a client says, "Every time I have to speak in public, I become afraid," then she is telling you about a set of past experiences or episodes in which the problem happened. The client is also implying that she expects the problem events to repeat themselves in the future. Most anxiety issues work like this. The anxious person is generating what is called a "future memory," a memory of something that has not yet taken place.

Explaining how memory works to clients by sharing information about research that shows how malleable memory is and how it can be influenced by unconscious processing has had a strong impact on our work with them. The mechanics of memory formation will be covered more in depth later on, but we have learned through our work that you can immediately begin to shift the client's expectations by saying something like:

> "Your unconscious is constantly pulling from all of your past experiences to know how to act and react in the moment. For instance, if I was bitten by a dog when I was younger, the fear and trauma of that event leaves a red flag in my brain. Our brain is a survival machine, and when an experience carries a strong negative emotional charge, the brain says, 'Remember this!' So, the next time I encounter a dog, the fear kicks in because my brain wants me to be on high alert and either freeze, fight, or better yet, run like hell.
>
> "So my brain triggers fear based on the red flag that the bite left. When I see another dog that senses my fear, and the dog growls, I get another dose of stress chemicals that reinforce

the message that dogs are a threat. And the next time I see a dog, my brain knows that fear is the proper response. I don't have to think about it; it's automatic. My brain figures that it's the proper response because it's what I've been doing, and I'm still alive, so it's a good strategy for survival."

That's how the brain works. It uses all the past examples of "dog equals danger" to create an unconscious, immediate reaction in the present. This stress response is responsible for keeping our species alive. Unfortunately, it is also responsible for many of the millions spent on therapy each year!

If a person who fears dogs changes some of these memories and experiences so that she remembers feeling comfortable and even confident with a dog in one memory and then affection in another, resourceful memories are added to the storehouse of memories that the unconscious has to draw from. Sometimes going into a relaxed state and imagining being saved by a Labrador, cuddling a puppy, or petting a pit bull goes a long way in influencing the amygdala.

Research says that whether people are remembering or imagining an event—even a fantasy about the future—the exact same parts of the brain light up. On a neurological level it doesn't matter to the brain whether it is accessing a real memory or one that's made up. In fact, the brain doesn't make the distinction between something that is strongly imagined and something that is actually taking place. It all adds to the choices of how to respond in the present moment.

This means that each time a client imagined a dog and was afraid, she reinforced the fear, but by having the client rehearse being comfortable or confident in the presence of a dog, her unconscious mind is given new options so that she will more likely have a neutral or even a positive response when next encountering a dog.

This is where a little explanation to a client goes a long way. We often generate new experiences in our clients during change work by changing the emotional impact of incidents, such as the example given about fear of dogs. Even though the client will be able to feel differently when imagining the triggers that had caused fear, a part of her is going to say, "Well, yeah; but that's not how it really happened!" So a basic understanding of how "the brain doesn't differentiate between the real and the created memories as far as our emotional reaction is concerned," changes everything for the client. Then, when we do re-imprinting or the Change Personal History patterns described below, our client has a way of understanding the change work that adds to the expectation of change, which of course, adds to the effectiveness of the session. Neuroscience provides the best metaphors for change.

Because the people who come to us are fascinated by the unconscious mind, explanations like the one just given become the vehicles for our interventions. We give clients something to hang the change on, and when expectation and belief about the ability to change is increased, the work is already halfway done.

Memory Reconsolidation

Memory reconsolidation is just a fancy name for the idea that each and every time a person remembers something, memory changes based on what is happening right then at the time the person does the remembering, rather than at the time the event took place.

It's as if the act of remembering lifts the memory out of the brain to be reprocessed and then puts it back with the new information added. This is startling to most people. We like to think that we remember things the way they happened and that we can trust our recall, but every time we remember something, we change the memory. Memory reconsolidation is an active and very complex internal process that pulls from many areas of the brain.

Understanding memory reconsolidation is one of the most important facets to understanding change work. It gives us a better grasp of how the patterns and techniques we know are effective work. So, when we ask clients to imagine having a sense of confidence while in a classroom or to pretend having a loving relationship with their mother, what we're actually doing is changing a memory and laying it down with added resources. Remember, this process is for the unconscious mind. Consciously, clients know that the new take on a memory is not how the remembered event actually happened, but unconsciously emotional flexibility is being added to the brain.

If you ask an eyewitness to a road accident, "How fast was the red car driving?" the witness will say something like, "It was going at 70 miles an hour!" even if no red car was there. As soon as you ask the question about the red car, the witness's memory about the road accident is re-consolidated, and the witness remembers a red car being there.

There is a lot of research on this. For example, in one study by Loftus and Palmer, participants were asked to look at a video of an accident and, afterwards, were asked to estimate how fast the cars in the video were going when they hit each other. The question was asked in a number of different ways, however, with the word "hit" being replaced by words such as "smashed" or "bumped." When the "witnesses" were asked how fast the cars were going when they "smashed" into each other, they gave a much higher estimate of speed than those "witnesses" who were asked how fast the cars were going when they "bumped" into each other. How the question was asked influenced the information that went back into the memory of the study participants. This is why attorneys are not allowed to ask leading questions in court and why they still do! [Loftus EF and Palmer JC. Reconstruction of automobile destruction: an example of the interaction between language and memory. *Journal of Verbal Learning and Verbal Behavior.* 1974; 13(50:585-9.]

Now, bear in mind that all Loftus and Palmer did was to ask questions with one word, "smashed," replaced by another word, "bumped." They weren't even asking the participants to vividly imagine something, nor were they seeking to elicit emotional states. Even so, this simple play on words was sufficient to prime the participants' conscious and unconscious responses.

In another study that took place in the week of the Challenger space shuttle disaster, participants were asked about where they were and what was happening around them when they heard about the incident and how they heard about it. Those same study participants where then asked the same questions nine months later and were also asked about how confident they were about the accuracy of their memory. Of course, they were all very confident because they thought, "How could I forget!" A quarter of the subjects gave very inconsistent answers, however; yet they were almost as confident in their memories as those who gave consistent answers. [McCloskey M, et al. Is there a special flashbulb-memory mechanism? *Journal of Experimental Psychology: General.* 1988;117(2):171-181.]

We used to think that "flashbulb memory," which is a memory with a very strong emotional reaction, was very accurate because it was burned into consciousness so strongly, but now we are finding that this not the case at all. The emotionality of flashbulb memory is burned in, but the details fade and change with new information because of reconsolidation. Interestingly, the professor who ran the Challenger experiment did so because of a peculiar memory reconsolidation episode that happened to him. He was relating an event that had happened to him when his assistant said, "No, that was me! That happened to me; you weren't even in town!" and the professor exclaimed, "That's impossible! I clearly remember . . . ." He couldn't believe how absolutely certain he was of a memory, that wasn't even his.

This is what happens. Memories get reconsolidated. Although we will swear that they are true, we trust our most updated memory, and the original version is lost.

Reconsolidation Using Re-Imprinting

As a change worker, you are probably familiar with some method of re-imprinting. Re-imprinting simply refers to taking clients back to an earlier experience, typically a childhood experience that took place during the "imprint" stage before the age of seven. The experience is then "changed"" by "gifting" resources to the "younger them" as well as perhaps to other people in the remembered scene.

With what we know now, you can begin to look at re-imprinting from the perspective of memory reconsolidation. So you may be working with someone who will say,

Client: "This all started when my father left, and I was six . . . ." [. . . and you'll see the client emotionally regress to that childhood state. The first rule is to dissociate the client from the problem state.]

Coach: "See that scene over there? There's that younger you on a small screen down across the room." [Point to one corner of the room. Using the small screen keeps the client from associating back into negative emotions.] You have all these resources, strengths, and emotions as an adult . . . . What resources would you like to send to that younger you?"

Client: Maybe some love so she feels safe.

Coach: And you know what it's like to feel love. When you spoke about your daughter earlier; well, I know you know love . . . ."

Client: Yes, I do. She is the love of my life.

Coach: And as you feel how much you love your daughter, now, imagine sending that younger you over there on that screen the same kind of love. Imagine it flowing over there so that she feels it and knows she's safe. And as she's receiving all of that, what are you noticing?

Client: She looks more relaxed. It's as if she knows this wasn't really about her.

Coach: That's right. And as she knows that and relaxes, feeling so much more resourceful, knowing she's loved, imagine floating into that memory and holding her close. Allow her to merge with you so she can grow up inside of you more resourceful, knowing she's loved.

Sometimes you can allow a client to send resources to the other people in the memory as well so the whole scene goes down differently. When the client in our example above is in a position to send some much-needed resources—maybe some strength or compassion—to another person, such as her mother, the emotional impact has many layers.

Once everyone in the scene is resourceful, and if it's appropriate, you can ask the client to float into the scene and feel how much better the experience feels. Obviously, it would not be appropriate to associate the client into certain memories even after everyone in the scene is resourceful: scenes of abuse, for example.

Alternatively, a good memory could be turned it into a fantastic one! One NLP pattern that we teach is called the Perfect

Parents pattern. This is a regression in which the client is taken to various events in childhood, including happy events, and the events are turned into fantastic events.

Reconsolidation Using Change Personal History

Change Personal History is a technique from NLP. It's a little like re-imprinting except that a number of memories can be worked on at the same time or one after another, and they can be from any period, including recent events, in the clients life. We typically use this process when a client has a recurring pattern that she wants to change.

We've already talked about how we can add resources to different memories, to build the storehouse of options, and how this can lead us to behave and react differently today. By doing the Change Personal History pattern, we can change a number of different memories at the same time, add resources, and even change beliefs that we have about ourselves or the world. By changing a number of memories at the same time, we increase the chances that the new feelings and new behaviors will generalize over a wider number of contexts.

So lebt's provide an example from one of our workshops:

Shawn: What would you like to change?

Mike: I get a bit touchy; I take things personally.

Shawn: You take things personally. So somebody says something, and it's about you?

Mike: Yes, it's like, "I can't believe you did that!"[As Mike says this, he begins to look a little angry. Now that he is associated into the problem state, Shawn will search Mike's memory for examples of times and places when Mike felt "touchy" in the past. Remember, state-dependent learning suggests that it is easier to find memories of an event when you are in the same state that you were in at that time.]

Shawn: Can you think of some times in your life, some events in your life when this feeling took place? Let's say, spread over a period of time, so . . . maybe teenage years, twenties, thirties . . . Can you pick three for me?

Mike: Yup.

Shawn: As you pick those three, can you put them in a time order in front of you? What is the title of the oldest one?

Mike: "I wasn't invited."

Shawn: "I wasn't invited." OK. What's the second one?

Mike: "Motherfucker."

Shawn: "I wasn't invited" and "Motherfucker." We'll say "MF" for the PG audience, how's that? What's the third one?

Mike: Family feud.

Shawn: "I wasn't invited," "MF" and "Family feud."

[Now we have three memories to play with and to change using the process of reconsolidation. When working with a real client, we would probably use between three and five memories. Using only three allows us to make the demonstration a little shorter.]

Shawn: You see those three scenes. One, two, three. What I want you to do is to take "I wasn't invited" and just expand it so you see that in front of you.

[Usually in the change personal history technique the coach will keep the pictures small in order to maintain the dissociation. In this case, Shawn wanted to use Mike's high levels of energy to create a positive state and, therefore, invited him to make the pictures bigger.]

Shawn: . . . And see the younger you in the picture. So, what's the resource you have now, maybe as a result of this class, that the younger you didn't have, but if the younger you had, would be different now?

Mike: Acceptance.

Shawn: Acceptance. OK, so for the benefit of the class, "acceptance" sounds very passive to me: "I wasn't invited, but I accept that . . . ." Is there anything else?

[As noted above, Shawn wanted to use Mike's high levels of energy to create a positive state. When finding an appropriate resource, it is often easier to match the "energy" of the negative state, so, for example, a high-energy idea, such as "excitement," might be better than a low-energy idea, such as "acceptance," to replace high-energy "anger." Of course, in making the side comment to the class, Shawn was also making it to Mike.]

Mike: Indifference?

Shawn: Acceptance and indifference . . . hmmm . . .

Mike: You're looking for something else . . .

Melissa: Well, think of those resources. Not only are they passive, there's almost a flatness to them. It doesn't have much of a hit, does it? If it were me, I would want a bit of cockiness . . .

Shawn: "I don't even want to go to the fucking party!"

Melissa: That, to me, has a little bit more energy. It gives you more power.

Shawn: What I would be feeling is this, I wasn't invited but I have my time. I could still do something else. I have choice, free choice, a sense of fun, a sense of excitement.

[Melissa and Shawn continue to invite Mike to find a higher energy state.]

Mike: But it doesn't solve the issue for me.

Shawn: Great! So what does solve it?

Mike: I guess if I could feel totally cool . . . [As Mike says this, he rolls his shoulders and takes on a little of the suggestion of "cockiness." Shawn decides to build the state a little more. Each time he repeats back Mike's words in what follows, he rolls his shoulders, uses the same tonality to pace the states Mike is in, and adds just a little more cockiness to lead the state higher.]

Shawn: You could feel totally cool! You see the picture, and you now have the ability to be totally cool. I would like you to give the ability to be totally cool to the younger Mike in the picture. And see how that is different now that Mike has the ability to be totally cool.

[Mike's posture straightens . . .]

Shawn: That's right! Now see Motherfucker in front of you. See the Mike in the MF picture. And we know Mike can be totally cool there now, but is there anything else in addition to being totally cool that you would like to give that Mike?

Mike: I think so. The ability to express a straightforward state! [Mike snaps his fingers . . . snap, snap.]

Shawn: I would like you to give "totally cool" to the younger Mike in the picture. And give the ability to express a straightforward state [snap, snap.] And notice how that's different . . .

Mike: A lot better. [At the point, Mike is smiling with high-energy.]

Shawn: Now, number three, Family Feud. You could give the younger Mike totally cool and you could give him [snap, snap.] Is there anything else that you would like to add to that?

Mike: Generosity. [As we review each of the memories, we add the resources that Mike has already identified, "totally cool' and "straightforward," but also give him the opportunity to add additional resources, in this case "generosity."]

Shawn: Being generous with your family—there's a concept! Generosity, totally cool, [snap snap] . . .

Mike: Straightforwardness.

Shawn: Give those to the younger Mike in the picture. Notice how that's different.

[As Mike looks at the pictures he is visualizing, he appears to be totally changed. To reinforce this change, , the principles of reconsolidation will be used by recalling each of the memories once again and adding even more resources. This additional resource will be the learnings that Mike has just acquired from going through the exercise the first time!]

Shawn: So Mike, you've just been through this exercise. So now take what you've just learned from this exercise and look at "I wasn't invited," and take what you've just learned now and give those learnings to the younger Mike in the picture. You've got that? [Shawn watches Mike looking at the picture and notices his posture and facial expression shift to be even more positive. He will now repeat the second round of reconsolidation with the rest of Mike's memories . . .] Go onto the second one. Take what you just learned in this exercise and give the learnings to the Mike over there [snap snap].

Mike: Very helpful.

Shawn: Very helpful indeed! Family feud, generosity, straightforwardness.

Mike: Much better. [Mike's attention is now completely on the imaginary pictures in front of him, as if he cannot see the class around him. This focus on his internal processing of memory is a kind of waking trance. Shawn offers Mike the opportunity to continue the work using his unconscious mind. This is often referred to as giving "process instruction."]

Shawn: From what you've just learned, from changing all that, look at this first memory: I wasn't invited. And you can continue unconsciously. Because each time you look, you learn something new. Now, what I would like you to consider is, how many events are taking place in New York that you were not invited to?

[laughter]

Mike: [Laughing] Hundreds and thousands of them!

In the above example, three events encapsulated the issue, spread over time. In the context of the first memory, we found an appropriate resource, gifted the resource, allowed the client (Mike) to see how his experience about an issue is now different. Then, we went to the next memory and gifted that resource, plus any additional resources that Mike identified . . . then onto the next memory . . . . Just take three memories and label them—don't get wrapped up in the client's story; just get the title. You don't need the story; the client has been telling it long enough.

Be aware that some people have a strong tendency to associate very quickly into memories. Associating too quickly and getting caught up in old emotional reactions is the basis for the problems of many of our clients. Direct them to visualize small pictures; it's harder to re-associate into a small, distant image than a large, close one. With a smaller, distant image, the client can have a more objective view of the problem: "That younger you down there. What do you have now that the younger you could have used back then?" In Mike's case, Shawn sought to keep hold of the energy of the anger and transform it into something more useful.

The more times the re-imprint can be reinforced, the better. Each time we re-imprint, or change personal history, we reconsolidate and we change the memory. Each time we change the memory, we make it harder for the client to return to how it originally was.

Melissa usually does this pattern while the client is in trance. A reason why you may want use the pattern this way is that trance always gives a client something to hang the change on. In other words, conversation-based change work exercises often are interesting and make the client feel good, but the client may walk away thinking, "Well, that was just imagining. How can that possibly work? I've spent my life imagining things." But she hasn't spent her life going into hypnosis, which still has an air of mystery about it, with the possibility of miraculous types of change. So, if you do the exercises described above in this chapter from inside of hypnosis, you will get a little more focus and a lot less conscious minded-conversation, chit-chat, and second-guessing from the client. A robust narrowing of attention is achieved.

More importantly, hypnosis becomes the driving force for the client's justification for the change. The client needs a way to understand and explain the change to herself and the people close to her. When a 10-minute change work pattern is done that just feels like pretending to the client—even a reaction that the client has had for years is changed, the change doesn't make cognitive sense to the client. She will say, "It's too easy! It can't possibly be that simple!" And that doubt doesn't help solidify the change. Trance opens up possibilities and gives the change worker a little bit more room to work with the client. Hypnosis is mysterious and ineffable to most people and can be the very thing that the conscious mind needs to explain rapid change.

The need for conscious understanding is why explaining reconsolidation and the unconscious influence of a reimagined past experience, as described at the beginning of this chapter, is a must. Never underestimate the power of the conscious mind to step all over a beautiful pattern.

You can also create change in a more cognitive way first and then repeat and reinforce it in trance. This allows for a more generative change. If you watch recent demonstrations by Richard Bandler, you will see him use this approach.

To reinforce change you can say, "Now, your unconscious can help you to understand what's different. What's important to you now?" And you will get different types of answers from the client's more open and inner focused state. So use hypnosis to reinforce conversational change work, giving the client a way to understand the change: "Now I've changed because I was hypnotized."

Certain clients will need the trance because of their belief that their problems are hard to fix. For these clients, some of the more rapid change processes are almost an insult to them.

They're highly invested in their problem; they've spent years and thousands of dollars on therapy. Simple change doesn't make sense to them and challenges their beliefs about themselves. Change through hypnosis becomes a way of explaining the unexplainable.

Five Types of Memory

Neuroscience identifies five different types of memory, each with a specific purpose. The first type of memory, which we already discussed, is working memory that takes the form of a movie or video loop that plays in the mind and has an audio soundtrack and a purpose. When you think about that lovely beach vacation you have planned, and you run it over in your mind, it's playing in your working memory. Working memory is becoming a topic of great interest in the educational world because it is, in many ways, the basis of learning.

The second type of memory, which we have also discussed above, is episodic memory. This is a memory of the specific sights and sounds that were seen and heard, as well as the emotions attached to an event. For example, when you remember the last time you went on vacation, you are accessing an episodic memory.

The third type of memory is semantic memory, which is memory of facts or things that you know to be true. For example, you may remember that you went to Washington DC on vacation. This is an example of an episodic memory. However, knowing that Washington DC is the capital of the United States is an example of a semantic memory.

It is thought that semantic memories start off as episodic memories; to have a semantic memory about Washington DC, you must have once heard or read that Washington DC is the capital of the United States. Over time, the semantic memory— the fact about something—becomes separated from the episodic memory, the event or events that created it. At that point, semantic memory memories stand alone as "facts".

The fourth type of memory is procedural memory, which refers to how we do something, such ride a bicycle. You don't need to remember a specific time—an episodic memory—when you rode a bicycle to remember how to ride one now. Also, procedural memory is not the same as semantic memory: "I know I can ride a bicycle." This is a semantic memory, but if you actually get on a bicycle and ride it, procedural memory is involved. Hence, the old joke, "Can you play the piano?" "I don't know; I've never tried."

The final type of memory is implicit memory, which we discuss in Chapter 4.

These different types of memories can overlap. Imagine that your friend asks whether you are free during the weekend. You know, as a matter of fact, that you are free. This is a semantic memory. So you tell her yes, and on Saturday, you both ride your bikes to Central Park using your procedural memories about bicycle riding. As you ride, you imagine stopping at the Boathouse in Central Park for a cold drink using your working memory. On the way, you see a red light and automatically stop using your implicit memory. In the evening, you look back on a pleasant day using your episodic memory.

Let's briefly review the Change Personal History demo in terms of the specific memories being accessed. We say to the client, "What do you want to work through?" And he says, "I take things personally." That's a semantic memory; it's in words. It's something he knows, or we should say, believes, about himself, but at this stage, the belief is separated from the actual episodic memories that created it. The easiest way to find these episodic memories is to take the client back into the emotional state that is associated with that belief and use that state to access the related episodic memories.

So the semantic memory (the belief) comes from episodic memories of specific things that took place. We want to find a number of those specific episodes to do the change work. Why? It's because it's more difficult to change something that's only semantic. It's not impossible, as we will see later in this book, but specific events are easier to address.

In the Change Personal History pattern, we're loading—or rather, reloading—these episodic memories, one by one, into working memory. We're changing the meaning, the title of the movie from, "I wasn't invited" to, "Totally cool" and then, we are creating a new semantic memory, which is the new title of the video. "Totally cool, straightforward, and generous."

And this is the key. The client's memories come with an emotional label, but the emotional label is something that the client feels in the here and now when she recalls the memory. The fundamental purpose of change work is to change this emotional label. Once you understand this, everything else is technique.

Working with Semantic Memory

Semantic memory refers to our memory of facts, for example Shawn knows that his birthday is September 21st. Gifts are welcome. A semantic memory may originate in one or more episodic memories: Shawn would have a birthday each year, and, amazingly, it was always on September 21st until he was able to extract from those experiences that his birthday is, was, and always will be on the same day of the year.

A semantic memory also can be thought of as a belief. Shawn believes all sorts things about himself and his capabilities, things that he can do and things that he can't do. He knows he is confident speaking in public and that he's not very good at baking cakes. These are semantic memories based on a whole series of episodic memories. Shawn doesn't need to remember all the times he's spoken in public to know that he can do so confidently; he just knows it.

Problematic episodic memories usually have a semantic component. The client is making some meaning out of her experience, otherwise she wouldn't have a problem, and the memory would fade. The unconscious mind is keeping the memory around because it wants to maintain the lesson until the semantic memory has been fully extracted. Note that that this is not always true. For example, phobias or post-traumatic stress disorder (PTSD) symptoms may not have a semantic component; they can be caused simply by stimulus followed by response, but in Mike's case in the Change Personal History demonstration, a semantic meaning arose out of the episodic memories. That meaning was, "I take things personally."

It is also important to understand that semantic memory may have become completely separated from the underlying experiences. In these cases, re-imprinting type patterns can't be utilized because the issue is not linked to specific episodic memories, so we can't ask, "When was the last time and place you experienced this?" Or, "When was the first time you experience this?" If we want to deal directly with the semantic memory, we have to change the meaning of the memory.

A reframe can change a semantic memory, which essentially is imbuing an episodic memory with meaning. There are two ways to reframe a memory. The first way is to change the meaning itself, and the second way is to keep the meaning the same but change the client's judgment of its meaning from "bad" to "good," which is often achieved by changing the context in which the experience took place. Here are examples of each.

Leslie Cameron-Bandler had a client whose presenting issue was that she became extremely upset by marks left on her carpet by her husband and children. Although not explicitly stated, this client was clearly making a meaning—a semantic memory—from her experiences of seeing the marks on the carpet. Perhaps the meaning was, "My husband and children do not care about me enough to keep the carpet clean," or something like that. So the marks on the carpet "meant" that the client was not loved, therefore no marks on the carpet would "mean" that she was loved

Looking at Leslie's change work case as if it were a demo, the client is asked to imagine a clean and unmarked carpet. It is suggested that a clean carpet "means" that the woman is alone—that her husband and children are no longer around. Once the client has accepted the idea that seeing an unmarked carpet means that she is alone, she is no longer able to hold onto the original problem. In effect, the footprints on the carpet now mean that she is not alone; she is surrounded by her family, by people she loves. The meaning, or semantic memory, has changed, and this type of intervention is, therefore, called a "meaning reframe."

In our second example, famed hypnotherapist Dr. Milton Erickson (1901-1980) has a family come to see him. The father is complaining about his daughter's behavior, saying that the daughter is "willful" and will not follow his instructions. Erickson reframes the father's attitude about the daughter's behavior by suggesting that a time will come when another man, who is not her father, will ask his daughter to "do something," and the father will be very pleased to have raised a willful daughter who is able to say no!

Within this new context, the daughter's willfulness becomes a positive asset, and the father is now able to tolerate his daughter saying no to him knowing that she will then be able to say no to other men. The semantic memory, i.e. the meaning of an idea, on one level stays, the same: the man's daughter is "willful," but her willfulness becomes acceptable—a virtue the man's daughter has—because it protects her from other men. In NLP, this is called a "context reframe," because the context through which the situation is viewed is changed.

Changing Semantic Memories Using Submodalities

Sometimes a client comes in with a belief but is not able to identify any events that led to it. Even if a semantic memory is completely separated from episodic memories of specific experiences, it can still be turned into a sensory experience by asking the client, "What do you experience when you think about that? What picture comes to mind? What do you feel in your body?" This internal picture or feeling becomes, in effect, a visual or kinesthetic "experience" representing the semantic memory. The picture that the client sees, or the feeling that she feels, "represents" the meaning. Changes can then be made in the "meaning" simply by changing the submodalities of the picture.

Submodalities are distinctions or qualities of experiences in the different sensory modalities of visual, auditory, kinesthetic, olfactory, and gustatory. To discover some submodalities of the client's visual system, ask whether the picture is clear or out of focus, in color or black and white, moving or a still, where it is in terms of location, whether it is framed or panoramic, associated or dissociated, and any other questions that provide finer details of the image. Auditory submodalities include volume, tonality, tempo, location of sound, and similar features. Kinesthetic submodalities might include location, sharpness, dullness, movement of feeling, temperature, etc. The same applies for all representational systems.

Understanding how changing these features changes our experiences is, in our opinion, one of the most important contributions to change work that NLP has made. We will get more into this later in the book, but for now, put your experimenter's cap on and try this:

Think of someone you love. Imagine seeing that person's face. Notice where the image is in your mind. Is it to the left, right, front and center? Is it in color? What else about it can you notice? Now imagine bringing the image closer and making it brighter. Notice how it feels when you do this. Now push the image farther away and make it small. Notice how this feels. Now bring the image back to where it feels good.

Interesting, right? Typically, when you make images brighter and bring them closer, you intensify emotions. Phobics usually have the image of what they are scared of—a snake, for example, large and close, right in front of their faces. Yikes! Shrinking the image down, turning it into a small black and white still shot, and moving it farther away will have a visible relaxing effect on the client.

So, when creating a sensory experience to work with in a client who cannot generate specific episodic memories, have the client manipulate the image, internal dialogue, or the physical sensations that go with the feeling that lets her know that she has a problem.

A good example of this is a case of generalized anxiety. The client is feeling anxious, but the anxiety doesn't seem to be attached to anything in particular. By asking the client where she feels the anxiety in her body and which way it is moving, we create a sensory experience in the moment that will become an episodic memory. We can then change the experience, for example, by asking the client to spin the feeling being experienced in the opposite direction, or we can turn the feeling into a metaphor and work within that to change the feeling. Here's an example:

Client: I'm feeling anxious.

Coach: Where is that feeling in your body?

Client: I feel it in my gut.

Coach: And that feeling in your gut. What is it like?

Client: It's like a swarm of bees or something.

Coach: And what has to happen to a swarm of bees to stop it?

Client: Well, I saw this show where they use smoke, and they all just fall asleep.

Coach: Close your eyes and imagine that happening.

Client: OK . . .

Coach: And what do you notice now?

Client: When I imagined them falling to sleep, the buzzing stopped and my stomach calmed down. How weird is that?

Coach: Pretty weird. But your unconscious mind is very symbolic, and so, you might be surprised how things can change . . .

We will cover many more ways to utilize submodalities in this book, with focus on the neuroscience underneath the interventions. For now, back to memory formation . . .

Long Term Memory Formation

For change work to be successful, the client has to remember to feel new emotions and enact the new behaviors on a long-term basis. We have to help the client replace one long-term memory with another, and, therefore, we have to understand how long-term memories are formed.

Long-term memories are memories that become hardwired into the brain. The wiring of the neurons becomes semi-permanent and does not simply fade over time. We say semi-permanent because of the principle of reconsolidation, but long-term memories remain as relatively stable as memories can be.

Creating long-term memories during change work is a two-step process. First, we pay attention to the new emotions and behaviors using our working memory. Second, if what we are paying attention to is deemed to be sufficiently important, it begins to be laid down into long-term memory by the hippocampus.

Let's talk about how we form memories, especially episodic memories, in more detail. For someone to form a memory, the person has to either have an external experience or load up the working memory with an internal experience. Remember, if we are working with internal experiences, we are using the working memory, which has a video loop, an audio loop, and a title or purpose (a director).

When we are using working memory, we have to lock these three pieces: visual, audio, and title, into place with dopamine. This is good dopamine, the dopamine of fun. We then have to pay attention to what will become the memory. Paying enough attention to something over enough time is called "attention density." If there is enough attention density and enough emotional energy involved in the experience, then a memory of the experience is pushed to a part of the brain called the hippocampus, where it is temporarily stored. Then, at night, during sleep and dream, the memory is replayed to the visual, auditory, and other sensory cortices. Over the course of years, the memory is ultimately stored as sensory information; that is, as pictures and sounds.

But before the imprinted experience is transferred into long-term memory, the experience first needs to be placed in working memory, locked in there with dopamine and attention density. If this does not occur, the memory isn't transferred to long-term memory.

The brain pays attention to something based on novelty, through repetition, by linking the experience to as many other experiences as possible—and using a lot of emotional content. This is how an experience is going to become a memory and be transferred to the hippocampus and, from there, move into long-term memory. This how your client is going to learn.

For example, Shawn's nephew James from the United Kingdom recently visited New York. James is an avid cricket player and had read about an English cricket player who attended off-season training with the New York Yankees. The story described how training with the baseball team gave the cricket player new insights into his own sport. James was fascinated with the story and, as a result, also become fascinated with baseball. By the end of his vacation, James had been to more games and knew more about baseball than most Americans. James was able to learn about baseball so easily because of his existing passion for cricket, the novelty of a cricket player training with a baseball team, and his ability to link the facts about baseball with what he already knew about cricket.

The hippocampus is responsible for the creation and storage of memories before they are transferred to the sensory portions of the neocortex. However, other than spatial memories of driving routes, most memories are not stored on a long-term basis in the hippocampus; they are stored in the relevant portion of the sensory cortex, but, if an experience is deemed to be sufficiently important (i.e., novel and emotionally charged), then it is temporarily stored in the hippocampus until a long-term storage space has been created.

To create this long-term storage, the hippocampus then begins to send the memory back to the sensory areas of the brain where it was originally generated; the visual portion of the memory is sent back to the visual cortex in the occipital lobe, the auditory part of the memory is sent back to the auditory regions of the brain in the temporal lobe, and so on. In this way, memories are split up and stored on a sensory basis. This transfer of memory from temporary storage in the hippocampus to permanent storage in the sensory cortex takes place over a long period of time. For the most part this process takes place while we are asleep.

Given that we are bombarded with information every day, and every moment of every day, how does the hippocampus know which experiences to store in long-term memory and which to discard? Remember, the hippocampus recognizes that experiences are worth remembering based on whether they are novel and also on the amount of emotional energy that they carry; the more emotionally charged the experience is, the more likely it will be laid down into long-term memory.

Application to Coaching

If a piece of change-work is tedious and boring for the client, it will not be laid down in long-term memory, and no permanent change will take place so it's vital to use elements such as humor and curiosity to make your sessions memorable and to link the change to things that the client is already interested in.

If you can get the client to laugh during the change work, the chance for change is much greater, with the learnings being laid down into long-term memory. So, associate the client into the positive aspects of the change and give yourself permission to be theatrical, energetic, mysterious, and otherwise entertaining when working with clients. You want your sessions to be filled with lots of memorable moments! We cannot overemphasize the importance of using positive emotions to create change in your clients!

Let's summarize the steps by which long-term memory formation takes place during and after change work.

Step 1: Focus the client's attention on the new state-behavior.

If your client is not focused on the change work, for example, if she is distracted, then it is highly unlikely that the changes will be laid down into long-term memory. The coach also needs to ramp up the client's level of focus by reminding her of the importance of the change, "Why do you want to make this change? Why is it important?"

Step 2: Get the client to give lots of attention to the new state and behavior.

This maximization of attention, called attention density, is vital to long-term memory formation. The client should use the whole of her working memory to focus on the new state-behavior without distractions, especially negative distractions. The client should see the change that she wants, hear the change that she wants, and name or label the change she wants to engage all parts of the working memory.

The coach needs to condition the new state-behavior using repetition. Repetition increases attention density.

Step 3: Make the new state and behavior novel and emotionally charged.

Long-term memory formation is aided by novelty and strong emotions. If there is little or no emotion attached to an experience, then it is very unlikely that the experience will be transferred to long-term memory. Generating strong emotions during a session is key to successful change work.

Step 4: Ensure that the client extracts a new and positive

semantic meaning from the new state and behavior.

As a result of her experience, the client will form an episodic memory, as long as you've 1) got her attention, 2) increased the attention density, and 3) generated novelty and strong emotions. However, the client is still capable of overriding the positive effects of the changes using her own semantic memory.

For example the client may say "Yes, but that was just in your office; real life is different!" By doing so, the client has attached a meaning to her experience in her semantic memory. That semantic memory will tend to override the positive effects of the episodic memory of change. This is why it's important to help the client make a positive meaning from her session. By describing how the exercise just done will change the way her brain will recode the memory shifts the meaning.

Step 5: Provide posthypnotic suggestions that the changes made will continue during the sleep cycle. If not practicing formal hypnosis, this can be accomplished by giving a brief explanation of how sleep solidifies change in the brain.

> "When you sleep and dream, these experiences will begin to be laid down in your long-term memory so the changes that you've made today will become even more solidified tonight because your unconscious continues processing and learning as you sleep."

Step 6: Offer the client opportunities to revisit the change after she has left your office.

Attention density is increased by repetition. The more opportunities the client has to revisit and practice the change the more likely the change will be transferred to her long-term memory. Give the client techniques to practice to keep her empowered and focused on the change. The fact that the changes are reinforced each time she uses these techniques should also be stressed so that the client takes advantage of priming via expectation.

Attention

ATTENTION!! This bit is REALLY IMPORTANT!!

Attention is the basis of learning, learning is the basis of memory, and creating new memories is the basis of change. Without attention, it all falls apart so knowing what attention is, how to get it, and what to do with it once we have it is vital.

SO PAY ATTENTION!!! While we talk more about attention density.

There are two types of attention, intrinsic and phasic. Intrinsic attention is paying attention to all the sensory information available to us at any one time. This could also be called mindfulness, and it is our evolutionary birthright, the state that allows us to pay attention to threats as they arise without the need to maintain a constant state of fearful guard. Unfortunately, it is a state that we often lose in the modern world of cell phones, stress, and rapid-fire information.

Being aware of what is going on at any given moment, particularly being aware of the feelings and emotions that we are experiencing, is the key to allowing us to change. This is why it is important to able to lead a client into a state of mindful awareness. This mindfulness state can be taught in many different ways, which we will cover later in the book. However, mindfulness is not so conducive to laying down long-term memories. For this, we need to create a state of focused or phasic attention. Phasic attention comes about when we pay particular attention to one experience, and during change work, we want our clients to pay close attention to what is going on. Therefore, one of the aims of your sessions should be to take clients through periods of focused or phasic attention and periods of wider or intrinsic attention.

A client will often begin a session in a state of "phasic attention" directed at the problem. She will tell you what is wrong in great detail, ignoring everything else. Once you have sufficient information about the problem, move from the original phasic state to an intrinsic state of attention to disassociate from the problem and identify resources. Then, you can lead the client back to a phasic state, this time focused on the solution.

There's many ways to achieve this move into intrinsic attention. Teaching the client how to move into an open-focus peripheral-vision state and the foreground/background pattern will be covered later in this book. Moving into intrinsic attention also occurs during the four-step coaching pattern that was covered in Chapter 2. Utilizing inductive and deductive questioning also shifts attention between phasic and intrinsic attentional states as it creates a very interesting trance. Here's an example of techniques that move the client into intrinsic attention:

Client: My son is going off to college, and I have this feeling of dread I can't seem to get rid of.

Coach: Where in your body do you feel that?

Client: In the pit of my stomach.

Coach: And what's everything else that you hadn't been feeling that's not that?

Client: Uh . . .

Coach: And what are some positive things you hadn't been

94

considering that you can now?

Client: I'm thinking of how excited he is and how hard he worked.

Coach: That's right. And as you feel how thinking of his excitement feels, now, mixed with love and future possibilities . . . what's everything else that's wonderful about your son that you weren't thinking of?

Client: Ah . . . so much . . . he's such an amazing kid.

Coach: And as you feel the truth in that, what has happened to that feeling you had in your stomach?

Client: It's changed. I feel more expansive when I think of how excited he is.

Paying Attention to Working Memory

Leading clients to pay attention to their internal mental processes, particularly to what's going on in the video and audio loops of their working memory, is important. Remember, the title of the movie is based on these loops even when our clients are not aware of them. Most clients are playing movies of events that have gone wrong in the past or events they are afraid will happen in the future, basically programming themselves for failure. For example, a client who is experiencing shyness when he wishes to speak to girls may be making a video loop of a particular girl's face as she rejects him, with an appropriate sneering soundtrack, with the name of the movie being something like "I must protect myself from embarrassment." It is easy to imagine how running this sort of movie could make someone feel shy! The coach can draw the client's attention to the video or audio loops that are playing in his mind so that he is better able to control and change them.

Here is an example:

Client: I have this horrible fear of flying.

Coach: As you're saying that, what did you just picture?

Client: I'm remembering a scene from the news about a plane crash. . .

[By continuing to direct the client's attention to her internal processes, she begins to realize that she is making negative images inside her head. From here the coach has a number of options, such as making the image smaller, more distant, or any other submodality manipulation that reduces the emotional attachment. In this example, the coach changes the content of the pictures.]

Coach: Ah, so you're seeing a scene from the news where there was a plane crash . . . And you're afraid of flying . . . Do you think those two things can be linked?

Client: [Laughing] I guess so! I didn't know I was doing it!

Coach: If you're going to make pictures in your head, they might as well be good ones. What pictures would be better for you to see?

Client: I can imagine getting home safely . . .

Coach: And what's it like when you do?

Client: That's much better!

Emotional Attention

The next ingredient in attention density is the emotional content of attention.

As a change worker, you will have noticed that your clients talk about feelings in either an associated or a dissociated manner. Some may say, "I feel angry" without really associating into that anger so the attention appears to be intellectual rather than emotional. Others talk about their feelings, and you can see the emotions reflected in the clients' faces and bodies as they describe them. So, why is there a difference in response when two different people are talking about the same emotion?

When the limbic system triggers a particular emotional response, it sends out two signals, one to the PFC, letting it know what is going on, and another signal to the body—to the adrenal and other glands in particular—telling the body to reset in an appropriate way. For example, if the emotion is fear, then the heart and respiratory rate will speed up, adrenaline and cortisol will be released, blood will be diverted from the digestive system to the major muscle groups in the arms and legs preparing for flight, and so on. As the body makes these changes, it begins to send signals back to the brain to inform it that the body is ready for action.

When a person is more used to tracking signals sent to the PFC by the limbic system, that person will tend to name the emotion "I feel angry" but may be dissociated from the emotion and not paying attention to the feelings it causes in the body. In contrast, when someone is paying more attention to the signals from the body, that person will be more physically associated with feelings but might not be so consciously or intellectually aware of the emotion, at least until it is pointed out.

The ability to move the client between these two different types of emotional attention depending on the stage of change work is useful.

Associating Into the Body Sense

Clients who find it difficult to access the emotions inside the body can be led to access them by drawing their attention to one bodily sensation and gently keeping their attention in their body until more details become available to them. This can be accomplished using "Clean Language" or similar language patterns.

Clean Language comprises a set of questions developed by James Lawley and Penny Tompkins and is based on the work of David Grove. The goal of these questions is to allow clients to more fully experience their own emotions and internal metaphors. Here is an example of Clean Language in practice:

Coach: And when you're feeling that, where do you feel that confidence in your body?

Client: Uh, I'm not sure, perhaps in my chest?

Coach: That's right, you're not sure. Perhaps it's in your chest, and when it may be in your chest is that inside or outside?

[The client has apparently guessed at the location of the body feeling by saying, "Perhaps in my chest." In fact, the body sensation exists throughout the body so it really does not matter where it starts. The next question, "Is that inside or outside?" is designed to begin to locate the feeling in a specific location in a way that is very easy for the client; normally the feeling will be inside the chest, although not always.]

Client: Inside.

Coach: That's right, it's inside your chest, and when confidence is inside your chest whereabouts inside your chest is confidence? [The coach continues to locate the feeling in a more specific location.]

Client: It's here . . . [The client touches the center of his chest.]

Coach: That's right. It's right there, and when confidence is in your chest, and it's right there, is there a size or shape of confidence? [Now that the client has identified a specific location for the feeling, the coach continues to keep the client's attention on the feeling by asking about other attributes such as size or shape.]

Client: It's like a ball, it's about this big [indicates the size of a grapefruit] . . .

Coach: So confidence is in your chest, it's right there, and is like a ball, and is there a color of that ball?

Client: It's red...

And so on. Remember, building feelings in this way tends to intensify them and therefore should generally only be done with positive feelings!

Dissociating from the Body Sense

When it is time to dissociate the client from the body sense so that she no longer directly experiences a negative emotion, the PFC becomes engaged when questions that use dissociating language are asked about the emotion. Dissociating language includes words such as "that" rather than "this" (*"That* feeling"), and past-perfect verbs: "That feeling you have felt," or "That feeling you had felt," or simply, "That feeling you had back then."

Reinforcing Change with Attention Density

Attention density is determined by a number of factors, the greatest being repetition. The more time we spend thinking about something—activating the emotions that fuel and are fueled by those thoughts—the more neurons and neural networks we recruit. Attention density is important because it activates Hebb's Law and causes neural circuits to wire together.

When a person thinks about a problem frequently, obsesses about it, tells everyone about it, and constantly considers how the problem impacts her life, she is strengthening the neural circuits that make up the issue. This type of thinking increases the attention density associated with the problem and will wire the problem more deeply within the mind. This is why it's crucial for change work clients to interrupt their patterns and why we arm them with countless ways to do so.

In the same way that attention density can create or increase a problem, it can also create and solidify change, but only if the client focuses her attention on the outcome and on any positive changes she has already achieved. We can encourage the client to do this by bringing her attention to any positive changes and emotions that happen during a session. For example, whenever we notice, from the client's body language and other nonverbal cues, that she is going into a more positive state, redirecting her attention to what she is feeling and picturing in that present positive moment solidifies the change. The more times the client experiences the change, the greater the attention density, and the more the change is reinforced.

As coaches, we can also link the change with other aspects of the client's life. This can be done by asking questions such as, "What will this change do for you? . . . How will you be as a person when you've made this change? . . . What are you believing about yourself now that you've made this change?. . . What other changes may occur in your life as a result of this change?" The coach can also ask more abstract questions such as, "What color is this new feeling?" This activates more neural networks around the outcome.

Asking the client to do homework associated with the change so that she continues to think about it and light up the relevant neural circuits also helps to solidify the change. We do this by providing tools that the client can use when she leaves the session. You can also ask the client to keep a journal of all the positive changes she notices daily.

We can also ask, "How do you know you have changed?" The coach may also challenge the client to prove that she has changed (note this should only be done after you are sure the change is solid, otherwise the client may begin to doubt that she has changed!).

Challenging the client to justify that she has indeed changed will also activate the client's semantic memory circuits.

Here is an example of some of the ways that attention density can be increased using repetition, "semantic meaning," and "linking." In this example, the client came in for anxiety felt while giving presentations at work. A new resource state of confidence was generated and anchored, and the coach now begins to do state collapse:

Coach: Tell me about another time you gave a presentation and felt anxious . . .

Client: There was a presentation I gave last year at our annual conference. It was a big room and I was looking at the audience and feeling anxious . . .

Coach: That's how you were then. And as you're feeling confident now [fires the anchor for confidence] take a look at the audience from where you're standing in the big room and notice how it's different now . . .

Client: Oh, that feels totally different!

Coach: Great! Tell me about another time . . .

Client: Well there was a big presentation I had to give to a client . . . .

[The coach continues in this way, asking about every presentation the client remembers having given and using the resource anchor to reconsolidate the memory with the new resource. This iterative process of looping through experiences one by one increases the attention density that the client is giving to the change. This is done until the client is no longer able to find more memories that carry the old feeling. At this point, the change has been generalized.]

Coach: Tell me about another time?

Client: I can't think of any . . .

Coach: Really? You told me it happened all the time?

Client: I can't think of anymore . . .

Coach: What about speeches or presentations you gave outside of work . . .

Client: I had to give a speech at a wedding, but as I think of that moment, it feels different.

[The coach continues to run the collapse using the resource anchor on all speeches and presentations and any similar occasions that the clients can find. This continues to build attention density.]

Coach: Tell me about another time . . .

Client: I can't. When I think of it, it doesn't make me anxious.

Coach: You mean it's changed already?

Client: Yes.

Coach: How do you know?

Client: It just feels different...

[The coach continues gently challenging in this way, again increasing attention density, this time by focusing the client's attention on the fact that she has changed.]

Coach: Now that you've made this change, how will your life be different?

The coach can continue to explore the implications of the change, which will again increase the attention density and further trigger Hebb's Law.

Learning and Sleep

Transferring learnings into long-term memory is a process that continues while we sleep. In fact, sleep is vital to the laying down of long-term memories. The mechanisms underlying this process are not fully understood, but what is known is that the experiences a person has throughout the day engage working memory. If the experiences are original and emotionally charged, they get stored in the hippocampus. When the person goes to sleep, the hippocampus replays the experiences and seeks to link them to other experiences so that, not only does the formation of long-term memories begin, but the experiences are also compared with what is already known, and the relationships with what is known are analyzed.

This replaying seems to take place during REM sleep and may be responsible for dreaming whereby dreams may be kaleidoscopic combinations of old and new memories that are being replayed and combined. When dreaming, a person experiences a mixture of what took place during the day all the associations the mind is making about what happened.

Once the hippocampus has had the opportunity to "replay" these experiences, sort them, consolidate them, and link them to what is already known, the hippocampus sends them back to the sensory cortex from which they came. Pictures are sent to the visual cortex, sounds to the auditory cortex, and so on. This process takes place during non-REM sleep, and the memory then becomes stored (over a period of time) as a linked network of all the sensory impressions that make up the memory, each sense stored in its own sensory cortex.

For example, suppose you meet a person who has a strong positive (or negative) impression on you. During sleep, the hippocampus will replay the image of the person's face, the sound of his or her name, and other sensory experiences that took place at the time. It will also begin to make links and associations. Perhaps this person reminded you of a childhood friend or wore a shirt similar to one you own . . . . The sensory impressions (such as the sight of the person's face, the sound of his or her name) are then "replayed" to the relevant sensory cortex. Ultimately, the memory becomes encoded in the visual and auditory cortices.

Sleep is vital to the laying down of long-term memories. You may have done the most wonderful piece of change work with the client, but much of the real change actually occurs while the client sleeps and dreams!

Application to Coaching

If we know that a client is best able to learn new ways of thinking-feeling-behaving (i.e., create a long-term memory) while sleeping, then the coaching session needs to be seen as a learning process that may start in the office but can stretch into the night and, indeed, into many days, months, and years ahead. Here are a few ideas for how to use this principle.

Create a set of posthypnotic suggestions that your client will sleep and dream and that once she dreams, she will review the learnings that have taken place during the session. Suggest that the unconscious process more deeply while the client sleeps and that the client will continue integrating changes made throughout the night.

An open loop related to the change work also can be created. Milton Erickson was a master of this and would suggest to clients that they would, perhaps, see a flash of color that would offer them insight into the change they were seeking. This type of posthypnotic suggestion leaves the client open to the change process long enough for it to be consolidated into long-term memory.

It also makes sense to provide your clients with "homework" that will continue to foster the change they are seeking. This may consist of "tapping" on certain issues using the Emotional Freedom Technique (EFT), bilateral stimulation, gratitude journaling, and so on. Again this sort of task will stimulate the mind long enough for the experiences of the clients to be laid down in long-term memory.

These learning patterns also happen whenever a person disengages from a thought process, whether a problem or something being learning, and does something else. A person can exercise, or simply take a break, as long as that person engages in a very different activity. We've all experienced having a part of the brain process a problem or the skill in the background, replaying it unconsciously, until we have an a-ha moment. Thus, this process doesn't necessarily only happen during deep sleep; the process is going on throughout the day as focus of attention shifts.

More Facts about Memory

Neuroscience provides other insights about memory that are of great significance to our roles as coaches. These insights include information about memory integration, memory distribution, and memory reconsolidation. These topics have been already briefly covered; however, memory integration, distribution, and reconsolidation are so vital to understanding how learning—and, therefore, change—takes place that we will spend a little more time on them. Because repetition is good for memory, the information is well worth going over again.

Memory integration refers to the process whereby new memories are integrated with existing memories.

Memory distribution refers to the concept that long-term memories are stored in the relevant sensory cortices: the visual portion of the memory is stored in the visual cortex, the auditory part of memory is stored in the auditory cortex, and so on.

Memory reconsolidation refers to the idea that each time a past event (an "episodic memory) is remembered, it is stored in a slightly different way depending on what else was in the mind at the time the memory was recalled. The thoughts being thought and the experiences being had when that memory is recalled become linked to it so that the next time the memory is recalled, those thoughts and experiences may also appear.

Memory Distribution

It was once believed that memories were localized in a particular part of the brain. For example, Wilder Penfield, who we mentioned in Chapter 1, began to map out brain regions during surgeries. Penfield would open up the patient's skull prior to surgery using local anesthetic. He would then stimulate certain portions of the brain to minimize damage to healthy brain areas during surgery. While the brain was being stimulated, the patient might report a very specific and detailed memory. Early neuroscience researchers, therefore, believed that the memory was localized in the particular area that responded to the stimulus. However, only a few of Penfield's patients reported this sort of localized memory trigger, and the effect was not replicated by later researchers. It is now known that memories are distributed throughout the brain. In fact, it is believed that memories are stored in the part of the sensory cortex that is appropriate for that portion of the memory so that memories of what is seen are stored in the visual cortex while memories of what is heard are stored in the auditory cortex and so on.

Because memories are distributed throughout the brain, each point in the brain at which the memory is stored becomes an access point for that memory. For example, as Marcel Proust (1871-1922) discovered, if you have a memory of eating madeleine biscuits with your aunt, you may be able to access that memory by thinking about your aunt's face, the sound of your aunt's voice, the smell of your aunt's house, or the taste of the madeleine biscuits. The more ways there are to access the memory, the more likely it is to pop into your mind. The reason we forget things is not necessarily because they've faded from memory; it may be that we have no way of accessing them. In contrast, you may have a client for whom nearly everything she sees and hears seems to remind her of a problem memory. In this case, you could say that the problem memory has a lot of sensory access points.

Two important areas to consider when thinking about memory distribution and its application to coaching are how negative experiences are stored and how we would like positive experiences to be stored. Negative experiences are stored and accessed according to what we see, hear, feel, taste, and smell at the time we had the experience. This can lead to the situation in which a person has a strong negative reaction to an environmental stimulus (something the person sees, or hears, or smells) that appears totally out of proportion to the stimulus itself.

We can see this happening with phobias in which someone has a very strong negative reaction to something that appears to be quite neutral to other people. The reason for the reaction may be that the stimulus for the trigger was present when a strongly negative experience (related to something else entirely) occurred. The stimulus became encoded in memory and serves as an access point to the past experience.

For example, suppose someone experiences intense anxiety when a red balloon is seen. It could be that the person had an intense negative experience sometime in the past when a red balloon was present. This experience was encoded in its entirety, and even though the red balloon has nothing to do with what happened, it still acts as a gateway to the negative experience. Now, whenever the person sees a red balloon, anxiety is felt. This may happen even though the person may not consciously remember the rest of the memory.

These negative experiences may also be accessible through the words that we use to describe them. Each of these words acts as an "anchor" for the memory.

If we, as change workers, wish to short-circuit these negative experiences in a client, then the more of these environmental and verbal triggers we address, the better. If we are able to apply positive resources to each and every one of the client's environmental, verbal, visual, or auditory triggers, it will be much more difficult for the client to ever access the negative experience again. However, if we address some of the triggers but leave others in place, the client may be able to access the negative state through one of the triggers that we did not address.

On the flip side, when we provide a client with a positive experience—for example, a positive resource—the more widely we can distribute this experience around the client's brain, the more easily the client will access it. We should, therefore, use the client's full range of sensory experience, as well as semantic experience (i.e., words and meaning), when installing a positive resource.

Sensory information should include what the client sees, hears, and, if possible, smells and tastes in the context in which she needs the resource. For example, if the client is seeking a sense of relaxed confidence when flying, it will be helpful if confidence is linked to seeing a plane as well as seeing the back of the seat in front of her, the sound of the aircraft engines, the feeling of air from the air vent, the smell of the airplane, and so on.

We should also ask what the positive experience means to the client, how it relates to other areas of her life, who she will be as a person when she has changed, and so on. Doing this will help the positive experience to be stored in many different areas of the brain and will allow it to be more easily accessed when the client needs it.

Memory Integration and Generalization

Memory integration refers to the idea that new memories become integrated with existing memories. Let's take a simple example: You see a dog in the street that barks at you. If the emotion is strong enough, you will remember the event. The experience then begins to become integrated with other memories. The barking dog will begin to be linked to other dogs that you have seen throughout your life.

You may draw "contrast links" between that barking dog and other dogs that did not bark at you, and you may come to the conclusion that just that specific dog is aggressive. On the other hand, "similarity links" may be drawn, generalizing the experience, and leading you to the conclusion that all dogs are dangerous. Either way, the memory will become integrated with what you already know about dogs.

The actual mechanism by which these limited generalizations ("some dogs") or global generalizations ("all dogs") takes place is controversial. Some researchers say they are made in the left temporal lobe. [Grabowski TJ, et al. A role for left temporal pole in the retrieval of words for unique entities. *Human Brain Mapping*. 2001;13(4):199-212.]

In any case, memory integration tends to lead to generalization, where experiences of a "similar sort" become linked, for example, in the case where an experience with a dog generalizes to "All dogs are aggressive" or "I'm afraid of all dogs." In that case, even if a person sees a dog that does not bark at her, she may treat that experience as the "exception to the rule."

To address this generalization, we, as coaches, generally use a technique that "dis-aggregates" experiences. We do this by asking the client, "tell me about a specific time and place it happened." This creates a contextual marker that makes the experience separate and unique. If the client says, "It happened on Tuesday at 3 o'clock," then the memory we are working with and, therefore, the neural network associated with it, is much smaller and a lot easier to deal because it involves one single pathway in a much larger network.

When we ask the client, "Tell me about a specific time and place this happened," it is very common for her to respond, "It happens all the time." This shows us that the brain has applied memory integration to link a large number of experiences together.

Linking the Problem to Positive Neural Networks

Memory integration can also be applied to positive change by linking the specific piece of change work to other positive neural networks.

For example, if the client has an experience of change during her office visit with you, then linking that experience of change to other experiences in which she has changed for the better can generalize into the idea that "I can change."

Memory Reconsolidation

Long-term memory is laid down in a process called memory consolidation. Although we think remembering something is like playing a DVD on which a past experience is stored, this couldn't be further than the truth. Remembering is a synthetic process that takes a dim and distorted memory of certain historical events and then synthesizes an experience around them that we call a "memory." As a result, each time we remember an event, the memory is slightly different from the time before. Most of the time, these changes have little or no significance. Perhaps we have a memory of a nice dinner in a restaurant and recall that the walls were red. We are discussing the dinner with a friend who tells us that the walls were blue, and the next time we remember the dinner, sure enough, we remember the walls being blue, not red. The suggestion that our friend gave us has subtly changed the memory, a process called re-consolidation.

Reconsolidation, as we've discussed, refers to the fact that we re-remember a memory each time we think about it, and each change we make in recollection is then re-stored in memory. Our memory can evolve over time. The more times we recall it, the more opportunities it has to change.

But sometimes the changes that we make in our memories can

111

be significant. For example, we may have had a conversation with a friend, which we remember as a pleasant experience. Later on, we discover that our friend has been spreading rumors about us behind our backs, and now, suddenly, all memory of the conversation changes and becomes much more negative.

The more the client thinks about her issue and the times in the past when she has experienced it, the stronger and more reinforced the memories become. The negative issue may also become linked to other areas of the client's life that really have nothing to do with it, simply because the client thinks about the issue in that location or context.

Reconsolidation and Extinction

The basic idea of change is that we attach a new neural pathway onto the trigger that used to lead to the problem. Once this new pathway is successfully installed, the section of the pathway representing the problem will begin to be pruned, it will become divorced from the context in which it used to occur. If it is not needed elsewhere, its neurons will ultimately begin to be used for other purposes. Of course, depending on the intensity of the problem and the amount of time that the client has been carrying it, the old problem pathway may be very well developed and, as a result, it may take some time to be pruned entirely!

Pattern Interrupts

Pathways can begin to be disrupted using "pattern interrupts." A pattern interrupt is simply an interruption as the client begins to run a familiar chain of thought. For example, suppose the client runs the following pattern: "I really want to quit smoking . . . . I've tried before, and it didn't work . . . . Everything I do goes wrong." As we have already mentioned many times, the more the client runs this pattern, the stronger it becomes.

Whenever the client thinks about quitting, she remembers the time she tried and failed, and this leads her to the semantic memory that, "Everything I do goes wrong!"

The coach can run a pattern interrupt on this to begin to break up the habitual chain of thought. Each time the client says "I really want to quit smoking . . . ." The coach will say "Stop! You really want to quit smoking, and how good will it feel when you do?"

In contrast to the process of reconsolidation, which leads to a reinforcement and stabilization of the memory, certain changes during reconsolidation can lead to a weakening of the memory. Ultimately, if the memory is weakened enough, it is lost in a process known as "memory extinction."

Much of the research on memory reconsolidation and extinction involves giving electric shocks to lab rats when they are in a certain environment. Cruel as this may be, it offers a close parallel to what many of our clients go through! They step into a particular context—perhaps they have to give a speech in public—and they get what amounts to an emotional electric shock. Research shows that exposing the same lab rats to the same environment, but excluding exposure to the electric shock leads to memory reconsolidation, consisting of memory without the shock, which ultimately leads to memory extinction [Suzuki A, et al. Memory reconsolidation and extinction have distinct temporal and biochemical signatures. *The Journal of Neuroscience*. 2004;24(20):4787-95.]

The principle of reconsolidation and extinction can be used to change episodic memories in a positive way. If we lead a client to recall a particular event but do so from the perspective of being more resourceful, then the resource will be reconsolidated. This creates a new memory, and the old memory will be subject to extinction. When the client remembers that event again, she will recall being more resourceful. This principle is the basis of NLP patterns such as Change Personal History, where the client's episodic memories change in a way that add more resources.

Memory reconsolidation also can be used to strengthen positive experiences. The more times the client remembers a positive experience, the more the memory of the experience is stabilized and strengthened. Simply asking the client to recall a positive experience following a break-state will strengthen the positive memory.

Forgetting Through Memory Extinction and Neuron Pruning

Neuron pruning refers to the process whereby neural networks that are no longer being used begin to decay. When this happens, we can truly say that a problem is over because the client's brain no longer contains the wiring that originally led to it.

Here we will discuss some ways that pruning can be promoted.

The Hidden Ability Strategy

A great way of beginning to prune the old neural network is to coopt it for another purpose. This is the basis of John Overdurf's "Hidden Ability" pattern, certain context reframes, and the six-step reframe of NLP.

In the hidden ability pattern, we find out—or guess—what the client must be good at to address the problem. This skill is likely to incorporate at least some of the problem network. By identifying this skill and using it to begin to solve the problem, this part of the problem neural network is coopted for other purposes.

For example, many clients who want to stop smoking have a

powerful ability to ignore or even rebel against social pressures. If this ability can be redirected towards rebelling against the manipulative advertising pressure of the cigarette manufacturer, then that portion of the network, which previously supported the smoking habit, will now support quitting.

The Forgetting-Power of Positive Thought

We all know people who, when they have bad experiences, set their intention to forget it. They say, "Hmph, this thing is not going to affect me; I'm going on my way." And they do. The inverse of this is someone who keeps ruminating and, in keeping it all very present in the mind, strengthens the very thing she wants to forget.

Evidence shows that the frontal lobe (i.e., the executive brain) can deliberately forget information. For example, research by Anderson and Green showed that subjects could deliberately forget words they had memorized [Anderson MC, et al. Neural systems underlying the suppression of unwanted memories. *Science*. 2004;303(5655):232-5.]

Therefore, giving a client conscious, or posthypnotic, commands suggesting the problem networks to disappear through lack of use may be effective. Perhaps a suggestion like this:

> "Research shows that when a neural network is no longer used, it begins to break apart. The neurons that form the network literally seek other things to do within your brain! You can accelerate this process by consciously instructing your mind to forget those old feelings and behaviors and instead pay attention to how you are different now. Once you've done this, you might find that you simply don't think of those old patterns anymore and allow

them to fade . . . ”

Recovery Strategies

The final way in which the pruning process can be accelerated is through the use of "recovery strategies." A recovery strategy allows the client to recover a resourceful state should she ever drop back into the problem. This strategy is installed by "chaining" anchors for states that can lead from the problem back to the resource.

In essence, a recovery strategy seeks to add a new neural network to the end of the problem network. In this case, if the client falls back into the problem, the following network is triggered: Trigger >Problem network >Recovery strategy >Positive state. So, even though the problem network continues to exist, it becomes part of a larger network that results in a positive-outcome state.

For example, a client visits to your office because she has performance anxiety about speaking in public. You anchor a positive resource of confidence onto the audience so that the client will feel confident whenever she gives a speech in public. By conditioning this new resource, you encourage the process of memory extinction. You also offer the client reframes and posthypnotic suggestions to encourage the PFC to reject the old way of responding. You also realize that to have performance anxiety, the client has to be very good at imagining what the audience is thinking. This is a "hidden ability" that the client can use to structure her speech to appeal to the audience. All the steps will tend to lead to either the pruning or the coopting of the old problem networks.

However, if the client has had performance anxiety for a long time, then the original (problem) neural networks will be very well-developed, and the process of pruning could take some time. So, attach new steps to the network so that the client recognizes when she is beginning to feel anxious, laughs at herself for this old way of being, and then begins to feel confident. The network is now: see audience > feel anxious >recognize "anxious" >laugh >feel confident. Obviously, you would also condition this change using repetition and the other elements of attention density that we have discussed.

Forgetting

We've said that there are two parts to coaching. One is learning, the other is forgetting. You want the client to learn something new and forget something old. You can think of the process like muscle use. When you're using muscles, you're building up muscle strength and density. The neural net associated with the muscle building become denser and thicker the more repetitive the muscle-building pattern is. It's fascinating. In contrast, what happens to muscles you don't use? A similar process is at work in memory extinction.

There are two ways of learning, bottom-up and top-down. In bottom-up learning, a person has an experience and learns from it. The learning is automatic and, in many ways, unconscious. In top-down learning, a person's conscious mind—that is, the person's PFC—says, "I want to learn from this experience," and the person pays attention with an intention to learn. As mentioned, research says that the opposite is also true; if a person puts intention on forgetting a certain list of words, she will forget more of the words than someone who doesn't intend to forget. In fact, research by Dr. Yi Zhong of Tsinghua University in China suggests that the brain forgets short-term memory on purpose so that it can update its map of the world. Admittedly, Dr. Zhong was experimenting on fruit flies! [Shuai, Y.C., et al. Forgetting is regulated through Rac activity in Drosophilia. *Cell* 2010; 140: 579-589].

If you want to forget a disturbing emotional experience, your

117

intention is to forget it. If you push that intention down, it will aid in the forgetting, but if you're saying over and again, "Oh my god, I just want to forget about this and not have this in my mind . . . ," but, at the same time, you continually recall the memory, then you won't forget it. You are, in fact, making the memory stronger because of the Quantum Zeno effect. "Trying" to forget in this way doesn't work; setting a forgetful intention does.

We don't expect you to memorize all of the information within this long chapter (although, you now understand exactly how your brain would be able to if you did). What is important is to appreciate that, on some level or another, your clients change when they forget their problems and remember the solutions they have always had. Also of importance is to remember there are so many ways to forget—and to remember—that we all have more choices for change than we may have realized!

Chapter 4: Working with Implicit Memory

Implicit memories are memories we don't know we have. Have you ever met someone who you distrusted but you didn't know why? It could be that the person unconsciously reminded you of someone who cheated you in the past. You don't know this consciously, but unconsciously and implicitly, you do.

Implicit memory doesn't seem to follow the same pathway, in terms of memory formation, as the rest of your memory does. Many neuroscientists theorize that implicit memory is primarily derived from neural systems that are "pre-semantic," meaning they track the structure of experience but not the meaning. In this sense, they are preverbal because to verbalize, at least at a higher level of abstraction, implies to make meaning.

So, implicit memory can be thought of as part of what happens before you become verbal, before you talk. This probably applies on both an individual basis and an evolutionary basis such that babies, as well as animals, are able to form implicit memories.

In any case, many implicit memories are formed very early in life. Clients may have reactions to events that don't really make sense, and the reaction may be a result of an implicit memory. Because the problem event goes back to a preverbal stage in the client's life and is encoded in memory without reference to language, when we ask the client what's going on, she will say that she doesn't know, and it may well be because she really doesn't! Clients literally do not have words to describe memories encoded from preverbal stages of life. Some therapists find that being able to sit in a caring and open state with their patients as they experience these emotions helps reduce the reactive nature of these types of memories.

Another way to change an emotional response in reference to something implicit is to generate a story or metaphor around the feeling. This engages the left hemisphere and begins to give verbal shape to the experience. For example, we can ask, "What is that like?"

Priming

Priming is a type of short-term implicit memory. It occurs when, with the experience of an event, the groundwork for a thought that will later emerge is laid down; however, "meaning" is not yet assigned to the experience when it occurs. Priming can occur verbally, using words that have an undetermined meaning or perhaps a number of possible meanings, or nonverbally, using pictures or other representations.

Let's consider a simple example: you know what a river is, don't you? You may have seen flowing—or overflowing—rivers, fast rivers with rapids, and slow meandering rivers, and when you think about the banks . . . What comes to mind?

Let's take another example. Following the recent financial meltdown, in which people lost their homes, a lot of attention was been paid to Wall Street financial practices, including new and complex financial instruments and derivatives, the marketing of which resulted in multimillion dollar bonuses to executives. When you think about the banks . . . What comes to mind?

In the first example, when you thought about "banks, it is likely that the banks of a river came to mind because you had been primed by all the talk about rivers. In the second example, when you thought about "banks," Wall Street banks probably came to mind because you had been primed think of financial institutions. Of course, you may have been primed in a different way by the exercise and had an "a-ha" moment of knowing what was going on . . .

Either way, you probably get the idea of priming now.

In one experiment on priming by John Bargh of Yale University, subjects were given word search puzzles. Embedded in the word search for the non-control group were words such as "Florida," "early bird special," and links to being old. The words in the word search for the control group were random. The experiment, however, involved measuring the amount of time it took the subjects to walk down a corridor to the lab versus back through the corridor from the lab. Those people who did the word search puzzle that included words related to being old (not the word "old" itself but words that implied aging), walked more slowly away from the lab than they did towards the lab. A bit of controversy exists about this specific research, but the demonstration of the priming effect is clear. [Bargh J.A., et al. Automaticity of Social Behavior: Direct effects of trait construct and stereotype activation on action. *Journal of Personality and Social Psychology*, 1996; Vol. 71, (No. 2): 230-244]

In another study led by Bargh, researchers unconsciously primed subjects using a scrambled sentence quiz for either the theme of politeness (using words such as "respect," "honor," "considerate," and so on), or of rudeness (using words such as "aggressively," "rude," and so on). A third group, which was the control group, was given neutral words. Then Bargh and his colleagues set up the subjects by saying, "This is the first part of the test. For the next part, just come and see me. I'll be in the next room, and I'll tell you where you need to go." [Bargh J.A., et al. Automaticity of Social Behavior: Direct effects of trait construct and stereotype activation on action. *Journal of Personality and Social Psychology*, 1996; Vol. 71, (No. 2): 230-244]

When each study subject entered the hallway and made his or her way toward the adjoining room, the subject found the experimenter in conversation with an associate. The experimenter was standing at a 45° angle in the doorway of the adjoining room and was partially facing the room and partially facing the hallway, making it relatively easy for a subject to walk over and interrupt the experimenter's conversation with the other person.

The conversation lasted up to 10 minutes from the time the subject approached the adjoining room to confront the experimenter, and the experimenter's associate timed how long it took each subject to become impatient and interrupt. The subjects who were primed with politeness waited pretty much for the full 10 minutes before stepping up to speak with the experimenter. Subjects in the group primed with rudeness were fuming while they waited, and the lapse time to interruption was much shorter—on average, about five minutes—compared with the subjects primed for patience.

How can we use the learnings from this experiment with our clients? As mentioned, including information from neuroscience research about how the brain can change in your pre-talk sets up the client's short-term implicit memory so the change work will be much easier to accomplish.

Some priming can be done while speaking to the client by

phone before she comes to the change work session. The client can also be given an intake form with questions that are designed to prime change. In addition to standard information, such as the client's name and contact details, the questions on the intake form can be directive tools for the outcome sought: how clients will know when they've reached the goal, and what they'll do to reward themselves when they've got the goal . . . . So the format is very much set up to prime the change.

Priming doesn't stop with words. Studies have been done in which subjects were primed by putting objects associated with business, such as a briefcase, a portfolio, and a pen, at the end of the table at which they were sitting, When the subjects were given the opportunity to split $10 with a partner, 66% set the proportion of distribution at $7:$3 in their favor. In contrast, nearly 100% of subjects in the control group set the distribution evenly: $5:$5. The conclusion drawn by researchers was that the presence of the briefcase "primed" a more businesslike attitude in subjects. [Kay AC, et al. Material priming: the influence of mundane physical objects on situational construal and competitive behavioral choice. *Organizational Behavior and Human Decision Processes.* 2004;95(1):83-96.]

These types of studies have been repeated, and it has been found that even the subtlest of influences, including change in temperature (as in asking a person to carry either a hot or iced coffee) and smell (as in infusing a room with a lemon-fresh scent) changes behavior. For example, a person's perception of another will be warmer if they are holding a warm cup of coffee or tea and colder if it's a cold drink, and a room that smells "lemon-fresh" can have the effect of making people behave in a tidier way. Thus, creating an office with an awareness of priming can give a client's unconscious a nudge toward making positive changes.

Priming Using the Interspersal Technique

Priming can be thought of as the basis of hypnotic embedded commands and the "interspersal" technique of hypnosis, developed by one of our favorite hypnotherapists, Dr. Milton Erickson.

There is a story about how Dr. Erickson helped relieve his secretary of a headache and helped her become more comfortable and relaxed by using the interspersal method. Dr. Erickson asked his secretary to type a report about a client in which he used phrases such as "I said to him, you are feeling relaxed," and "the more comfortable you feel, the easier it becomes to absorb this information on an unconscious level." As the secretary typed out the report, she began to feel completely relaxed, and all traces of her headache disappeared.

By embedding commands, such as "feel confident," or "you are relaxing," we prime the client's brain in the direction of confidence and relaxation. To aid in multilevel communication, we teach our students to use a slightly different tonality when embedding suggestions. The use of hidden metaphors or stories that we tell before the session officially begins and that contain hidden commands and suggestions can have priming effects on clients by creating short-term implicit memories.

We tend to use some of the explanations for neuroplasticity and reconsolidation as fantastic opportunities to educate, prime, and set an all-around state of expectation in our clients. By embedding positive suggestions for change inside broader descriptions of change, we are priming beliefs as well as behaviors. You may wish to create your own set of metaphors around subjects such as:

- Everything changes
- Learning is easy
- Relaxation

- Confidence

And so on . . .

The more explicit the stories are, the greater the chance that the client will consciously reject the ideas that the stories are intended to offer. Remember, research has shown that simply reading mixed-up sentences with words associated with old age, politeness, or rudeness could affect a study subject's behavior. No direct suggestion was given to the subject to feel old or behave rudely.

Consider the following contrasting pre-frames on the theme that everything changes:

1. Explicit: I find it very easy to change my habits, and you can too!

2. Implicit: I read a fascinating article on the brain's ability to rewire old patterns.

The first example is very explicit, and the client may reject its message. The second example is more implicit and should create a priming effect in the client.

Beliefs and Values as Implicit Memories

We may hold our beliefs and values explicitly, as semantic memories. We have already covered some ways to address and change these if they are limiting the client. However, implicit memories can also exist as "implicit beliefs," such as the belief that "I can't do this," or "I am a failure," and so on. In this case, the beliefs may only become accessed when the client is in the context in which she experiences the problem. For example she may believe herself to be a perfectly capable person, but when something goes wrong with her computer, she may adopt an implicit belief of helplessness. At this point, her neural circuitry is acting in accordance with the implicit memory that "I can't do this."

Implicit memories such as these may arise from childhood experiences, or imprints, perhaps related to what the client was told by her parents or teachers. Indeed many of our beliefs and values may be implicit: we believe something, but we are not explicitly aware that we do. These beliefs can be extremely empowering or else disempowering, in part, because they are implicit rather than explicit and, therefore, are difficult for us to consciously challenge.

One of the important skills you must develop as a coach is to be able to hear "beneath" what the client is saying to discover the implicit limiting beliefs. Once a coach is aware of an implicit belief, she can associate the client into the problem situation and then simply ask the client, "What are you believing about yourself and the world?" Chances are that, at this stage, the client will be able to recognize the belief as something that she holds to be true. At this point, the belief becomes explicit, and the client may be able to challenge it. In any case, the belief becomes a semantic memory and can be dealt with using the techniques described in the section on semantic memories.

If all else fails, implicit beliefs can also be addressed by trusting the power of the unconscious mind. Using "process instruction," by instructing the client's unconscious to "Make any and all changes that are required to fully and completely absorb and integrate the changes that have taken place," gives the unconscious mind the opportunity to change any implicit memories that may be involved in the problem.

Chapter 5: Mirror Neurons

We have social brains that are wired for mimicry. We are always learning from other people, connected in ways we are just beginning to explore. This can be seen when interacting with a baby. If you stick your tongue out at a brand new baby, the baby will stick her tongue out back at you. Whenever a parent is trying to feed a baby, what does the parent do? The parent opens his or her mouth because, then, the baby opens her mouth in response. This example shows mirror neurons in action.

You've probably heard of mirror neurons. Along with the idea that a person can rewire his or her brain, ideas about mirror neurons have made their way from the labs of neuroscientists to popular awareness. If you haven't heard of mirror neurons, don't worry; in this chapter we will be talking about how useful they can be in change work. Although there is still some debate about the reasons why mirror neurons do what they do and how they do it, mirror neurons do explain a great deal about human behavior.

Mirror neurons are designed to allow you to experience the physicality, emotions, and the thoughts of other people. When you see another person, your mirror neurons create an internal model of that person. This helps build rapport, promote empathy, and "mind-read" the other person so you can begin to predict what that person is thinking and what she will do.

Research led by Giacomo Rizzolatti, of the University of Parma in Italy, discovered mirror neurons in the 1980s. The discovery was a major breakthrough in neuroscience, the implications of which are still unfolding. Like the discovery of penicillin and many other great scientific discoveries, the findings of Rizzolatti and colleagues were due to an experimental mistake. You can read a fascinating account of the discovery of mirror neurons in Marco Iacoboni's book Mirroring People: The Science of Empathy and How We Connect with Others [New York: Picador. 2009].

Rizzolatti's team was scanning the brains of monkeys as the monkeys performed tasks and were rewarded with pieces of banana. —Or perhaps the monkeys were training the researchers to feed them bananas in exchange for performing some meaningless task. Whichever way the research was going, when the scientists took a break from the experiment, one of the researchers reached for and picked up a banana. As he did so, the research team noticed that, as the monkeys observed the researcher pick up a banana while their brains were being scanned, the same neural circuits fired in them as those that fired when the monkeys themselves reached for and picked up bananas.

The researchers asked themselves, "How does that work? How does a monkey's brain fire off as if it picked up a piece of banana just because the monkey saw a researcher reach for one?" As a result, they identified the specific neurons that were responsible, neurons that we now call mirror neurons.

You're definitely already familiar with mirror neurons on a kinesthetic level. Melissa loves watching people watch a football game. You can see the clenched jaws, tight fists, and the body braced for a hit. Or for a gentler example, if you've ever watched a sporting event that you were very interested in—perhaps watching a player serve at the US Open Tennis Championship—you'll be familiar with the feeling that it is almost you who's playing the game. You can actually feel your body begin to respond as if it, too, were playing tennis.

It is important to understand that different neurons are at work when you are feeling yourself swinging a tennis racket because you happen to see one and feeling yourself swinging a tennis racket because you see your favorite tennis player swinging a racket. When you see an object that you could pick up and manipulate, such as a tennis racket, your brain is using a cell known as a "canonical neuron," but when you see actions performed by another person that you can do too, your brain is using mirror neurons.

Mirror neurons come in various flavors, depending on the exact purpose. Rizzolatti and his team of researchers and others elsewhere have carried out extensive experiments to determine exactly when and how mirror neuron's fire, although these subtle differences are outside the scope of this book, the important point is that mirror neurons can be used to model the behavior and feelings of another person.

The research on mirror neurons also shows that they respond to sounds. In the case of the monkeys, the mirror neurons would respond to sounds such as the breaking open of peanut shells. Similar research, which is in an early stage of development, has been extended to humans, who, it's been found, respond not only to environmental sounds, but also to voice tonality [Gazzola V., et al. Empathy and the somatic auditory mirror system in humans. *Current Biology*, 16: 1824-1829].

Researchers have shown that different sets of mirror neurons will fire depending on the perceived intention over the action observed. If this sounds confusing, let's clarify it with a brief example. Suppose you see Shawn reaching for a teacup, which would certainly be possible if you are in his apartment at breakfast time. You may be thinking, "Shawn is reaching for a teacup; he must be about to sip his tea." But wait; there are several interpretations for his action. For example, he might be about to make a cup of tea, or he might have already drunk his cup of tea and be about to wash the dishes. Research indicates that the context in which Shawn picks up the cup is going to be reflected in the precise mirror neuron's that fire, tea drinking neurons, tea-making neurons, or dishwashing neurons.

Perhaps most importantly for our current discussion, mirror neurons allow us to feel the emotions of others. This, of course, is what is called "empathy," although prior to the discovery of mirror neurons, the mechanism that underlies empathy was somewhat mysterious. A person can feel empathy even if no other person is present. For example, if you look at a photograph of someone who is smiling, laughing, or frowning, then your face will tend to take on that expression as well.

Mirror neurons make up 30% of brain cells of certain parts of the brain. Think about it. Almost a third of your experience in certain parts of your brain depends on the experience of other people around you. This is how we're able to feel someone else's pain even when we don't intend to. Hollywood has been banking on mirror neurons since the beginning of cinema. And don't get the authors started on the mirror neurons of teenagers playing violent video games . . .

The action of mirror neurons has two amazing implications for us as coaches. First, if we mirror our clients naturally, we're going to have greater rapport. Research suggests that the biggest factor in determining the success of a coaching or therapeutic relationship is the degree of rapport between the coach and the client. The greater the rapport, the more effective the coaching.

And yet it is very difficult to generate rapport on a conscious basis. If you consciously try to mirror your clients, you'll spend all your time and energy doing so, and your clients will most likely pick up this "trying" and be annoyed. One of the fastest ways to interfere with an unconscious ability is to try to make it conscious. Just ask an athlete to explain in detail what they are doing and you will mess with her game, for sure.

The beauty is that you come equipped with mirror neurons specifically designed to allow you to unconsciously build rapport with your clients! If you sit with your clients in a relaxed, open state with positive intentions, your mirror neurons will do the rest. This will allow you to lead your clients in more positive directions.

The second implication related to the activity of mirror neurons is that it enables us to share our states with a client. If we're going for a state of confidence in our client, and we feel the state of confidence first, then the mirror neurons of the client will begin to fire off and take her into a state of confidence as well. Your confidence speaks directly to a client's unconscious mind, which is directly affecting the different areas of her brain through mirror neurons. Your flexibility will translate to her flexibility. The value of mirroring is not just a theory anymore; we can see it. We know how the brain reads the nonverbal cues enough to feel empathy and sympathy. That's the resonant circuitry we're talking about.

Another important point is to closely pay attention to the gestures and nonverbal markers of the client's resource state. Once you see how she looks when she thinks of the outcome she wants, then you, as the coach, should mirror that back. Wear the client's confidence, relief, or whatever she says she wants to feel so that you hold it constant. Simply ask the client how she wants to feel or what it will feel like when she has solved the issue, and she will show you through facial expressions, gestures, tonality, and tempo. When you hold and mirror the client's nonverbal communication, you're making her own unconscious system of confidence or outcome state more explicit.

This is exercising our mirror neurons. We always emphasize that the change worker get into a trance state when doing any kind of trance work with a client. This keeps all of your nonverbal communication congruent with the emotional states you are seeking to guide your client into.

There are other ways to use this rapport-connection once it is established. If you see the client falling back into the problem, do a pattern interrupt. The effect of mirror neurons is so strong that deliberately violating the mirroring process creates a pattern interrupt that can stop the client's thought process in its tracks. This pattern interrupt can be highly beneficial during the coaching process whenever the client dives back into the negative story because the client doesn't have to think about stopping. She's going to stop automatically and interrupt the pattern in her brain, like flicking a switch.

To do a pattern interrupt, you could suddenly raise a hand, palm towards your client, and straighten your spine while the client is in mid-thought. This thought will be immediately and irrevocably interrupted. If the pattern interrupt is done enough times, it will become hardwired into the client's thought processes, and the old pattern will be broken. An auditory component can be added by saying, "Stop!" with sharp tonality.

Flexibility is key. When you realize that we are always communicating on many levels, you begin to become more aware of your own states. The fact that knowing how you feel about the client, her ability to change, and your ability to help her influences the outcome should reinforce the importance of inner state management. All of these things are connecting, literally, to their brain.

Often-quoted research indicates that 55% of our communication is body language, 38% is auditory (our tone of voice and so on), and 7% are words. Although this research is dated and these numbers are at best highly contextual, it is certainly true that the actual words we speak carry a relatively small amount of the total message we're sending.

Nonverbal communication leaks out in more ways than can be controlled. Your beliefs about the client, yourself, and the change work being done will influence your gestures, facial expression, and tone of voice so that building rapport has got to start inside of you, the practitioner. We are taking in millions of bits of information unconsciously, yet we can be consciously aware of about 40 of those bits. So, when you realize all that the client is getting from you unconsciously, it makes sense to do what you can to increase the positive messages you're sending.

If you can't see a client as being resourceful and as having the ability to heal or change, then refer her to someone who can. If you don't see, feel, and believe her to be resourceful, then 93% of you is not on her side. Even if you're saying all the right things, a client will unconsciously know how you're feeling. Your tonality, body language, and brain are giving you away.

Chapter 6: The Eyes as Part of the Brain

According to neuroscientists, the optic nerve and the retina of the eye actually form part of the brain. The retina of a fetus starts out being a part of the brain and grows out on neural stalks to become the eyes. This means that the eyes are the only part of the brain that we can physically control. You might want to try that now. Look to the right and then to the left, being aware that you are actually moving parts of your brain around!

As sense organs, the eyes are amazingly controllable. We can move them around and change our focus from near to far and back again. We can intently focus on something using foveal vision, or we can expand our vision out using peripheral vision, and when in peripheral vision, we can shift our attention within our visual field without moving our eyes. Therefore, our eyes present us with a wonderful option to specifically control our mental input. And we do get what we focus on!

Eyes are designed with a small central area called the fovea. The fovea is designed to see detail and represents a very clear picture of a very small part of the world. In the fovea, each light sensitive cell is connected to its own neuron leading into the optic nerve, giving fantastic resolution. The rest of the peripheral visual field is made up of a much less detailed picture, one that primarily tracks movement. In fact, in the periphery, up to 100 light-sensitive cells service each neuron. This makes the neurons extremely sensitive to low light but gives very poor resolution.

However, our brains are so good at constructing our visual reality that we believe our peripheral vision also provides an accurate picture of the world. It was only when neuroscientists were able to conduct detailed experiments on peripheral vision that they realized the extent to which a person's peripheral visual field is actually being created by the brain rather than the eyes.

As you're reading now, you are using foveal vision because you're looking at these words. As you are reading these words, you probably think that the rest of the page looks clear as well. Think again. Your peripheral vision is too blurry for reading so only the words you focus on are clear and all the rest is, well, an illusion of clarity.

You probably also think, as you're reading this book, that you can see the rest of the room pretty well with your peripheral vision, but, in fact, you can't. It's a blur, but your brain is creating an impression in your mind that you can see the rest of the room clearly. It's making it up. Your brain is amazing in its ability to create your reality.

If you need a demonstration of how your brain actively makes up what you see, consider your blind spot, a portion of the retina where the optic nerve leaves the eye that doesn't have light receptors. Experiencing your blind spot is easy. Simply take a piece of paper and draw two dots about three inches apart. Now, close your left eye and look at the left dot with your right eye. Move the paper slowly toward and away—maybe by six inches—from your eye. The right dot is going to disappear as you continue focusing on the left dot. It disappears at just the point it passes into the visual field of your blind spot, where there are no light receptors.

But here's the million dollar question: What is it that you see when that dot disappears? You see the page, right? Whatever you're seeing in that spot is being created by your brain. The unconscious mind simply guesses at what it thinks must be there and fills it in—in this case, more white paper.

Your unconscious mind does a damn good job of making things up most of the time. If you cover one eye and look around the room, a portion of what you're seeing is filled in by your brain, which is extrapolating from what's around it, saying, "I'll just assume it's the same as the rest of the background." Your brain does that job because it likes cohesion. So, as long as you don't see big gaping holes in your vision, you know that your brain is making stuff up for you.

Because our eyes are designed to focus on what is important, and we tend to focus our attention on our problems, we come to believe that our problems are important. We already discussed the Quantum Zeno Effect, which is the principle that what we focus on tends to persist so this creates a vicious circle of experiencing a problem, focusing on the problem, and having that problem persist.

Application to Coaching

When our clients have a problem, we know that the solution doesn't exist where the clients have been focusing their attention. If the solution was there, a client probably would have found it already. Ultimately, coaching consists of drawing the client's attention to something new, a new piece of information. One way of doing this is to use our natural tendency to switch between foveal and peripheral vision. In fact, our left hemisphere tends to focus on the foveal portion of the visual field and the right hemisphere on the peripheral portion of the visual field.

Exercise One: Foreground-Background Switch

Think of the situation that is causing you a problem, perhaps an unwanted feeling. Associate back into the situation and notice what you are paying attention to visually. Notice a specific detail of that thing you're paying attention to. Let's call that detail the "foreground" and everything else the "background."

In working with a client, you can guide the client into allowing the foreground to move into the background while the background moves into the foreground. Do this a few times, and you will find the emotional reactivity to the problem changes. Neurologically speaking, this exercise involves switching from foveal vision to peripheral vision and, at the same time, from left-brain to right-brain.

Remember, there are two types of attention, intrinsic attention, which is basically peripheral vision, and phasic attention, which is foveal vision. We discussed how we most likely survived as a species by utilizing intrinsic attention most of the time because we didn't know where danger was going to come from. Intrinsic attention tracks movement and keeps us in a more open, aware state. It activates the parasympathetic nervous system.

But when we find something very interesting or threatening, focus narrows, and we have phasic attention. This activates the stress response and keeps us alive. Think about how your clients describe trigger moments. They talk about tunnel vision or the walls collapsing in. That's foveal vision. It was meant to be something we phase in and out of to keep us safe. Unfortunately, we seem to have cultivated it as a constant habituated state.

Exercise Two: Peripheral Vision

The "Stop the World" state, also called "open focus" or "peripheral vision," involves going into the peripheral vision state when you are actually in a situation that would normally cause your problem, such as an unwanted feeling. The Stop the World state can be practiced and anchored so that it will be available when your client needs it.

To lead your client into the Stop the world state, have the client pick a spot or focal point to stare at. While she is continuing to look at that spot, guide her to slowly expand her peripheral vision to include all the space around the spot. Then, lead the client to expand vision even further, to the sides, all the way up to the ceiling, and down to the floor. Expand it even more, allowing the client's visual field to open, and ask her to imagine becoming aware of the space behind her.

This might feel strange at first but after practicing three or four times the client will notice a general calm come over her mind and body. She may also realize that her internal dialogue has stopped. This is what Carlos Castaneda called "Stopping the World." Melissa teaches it to clients who have anxiety because it allows them to move awareness from the inside out.

The great thing about this technique is that it can be done anywhere, anytime. With practice, it becomes an easy way to change emotional states.

We can also teach clients to blend the foveal and peripheral states to create a more open focus state. Les Fehmi covers a lot of interesting research on this in his book The Open-Focus Brain: Harnessing the Power of Attention to Heal Mind and Body [Boston: Trumpeter Books. 2007.] By being able to guide your clients into this state of awareness, you create a synchronous, alpha brainwave pattern that has many different benefits.

One great benefit of open focus is that it builds of flexibility in the brain's ability to strengthen different neural networks associated with attention and focus. Open focus has also been shown to increase calm in the amygdala and decrease emotional reactivity.

Once the client is used to switching vision from foreground to background, have the client practice focusing on both at the same time. One way to do this is to lead the client to pay attention to space and not objects. This creates a softer, more inclusive state.

In foveal vision, it's as if the eyes latch onto things in a way similar to grabbing an object. This type of focusing is linked to the sympathetic arousal of the fight or flight response. Focusing awareness on the space around an object makes it very difficult to grab onto objects, and so we relax into the widening out of awareness.

Try this exercise: Once you know how the state feels, it will be easier to guide your clients into it. Hold up your hand, palm facing you, as you soften your gaze and focus on the space between your fingers. Just allow your visual field to expand a bit more and be aware of the space around the hand as well as the space between your fingers. Allow yourself to notice all of this as if you could be aware of the space *through* the hand.

Widen out the space so that you are aware of the space around your arm. While remaining aware of all the space between your fingers, around, and through that hand, become aware of the space between your eyes and your hand. Next, become aware of the space between your hand and your knee, your legs . . . allow it all to blend into an awareness of space.

Interesting? What's happening in your brain when you do that, according to Les Fehmi, is an alpha brainwave state, but it's synchronized; both hemispheres are getting the wave in equal measure. This exercise encourages a more cohesive alpha-wave state than the usual pattern of slipping in and out of alpha.

It's like taking your brain to the gym. Open focus cultivates flexibility by engaging a very different type of seeing than the foveal, stress-related collapse-in that most people are used to. Open focus is an open state that reduces chronic stress. We instruct our clients to practice it daily, and they report a more general sense of calm from the practice.

We experience space very differently from other things we set to memory. If we have a memory of a space—for example, of moving around a city—it's stored in a different part of the hippocampus than most other memories. The internal map of your city is stored in the right upper hippocampus, and this is known, in part, through study of the brains of London taxi drivers. London is not an easy place to navigate . . . .Streets might begin going north-south but then bend and flex and end up going east-west so it's easy to get lost. If you're a taxi driver in London, you have to know the streets. It's obligatory. It's Knowledge with a capital K. So, taxi drivers spend a year or two riding a scooter around just to learn the streets. As they do, the part of their brain devoted to navigation grows in size like flexing strengthens a muscle.

By the way, the research on London taxi drivers is a perfect example of neuroplasticity in which cell density—the connections and dendrites—thickens from use. Discussing this research, therefore, may be useful when explaining neuroplasticity to your clients.

So, space can be very important, and because memories about space are stored differently in the brain than other memories, adding spatial awareness exercises to your change work can be interesting. The open-focus exercise above is very good for clients who have focusing issues.

We love exercises that use peripheral vision because, as we've said, it stops internal dialogue. When we teach such exercises to our clients, we use the triggers of the clients as the focal point that they then expand out of. This exercise is an excellent pattern interrupt because it's hard to keep the anxiety—or whatever the problem is—going without the internal dialogue that supports it.

The Visual Cortex and Submodalities

How does the brain see? Vision is, by far, the largest part of your sensory experience. A large portion of your brain is for visual processing because visual processing is so complicated for our brains to construct. The big test for scientists working in the field of artificial intelligence is whether they can build a robot that can find its way out of a room through a door. For now, the general answer is no, or at least, not very well, and the reason is because vision is so complex.

While vision feels passive, like looking through a video camera, it's really an active process. When people have been blind and then get reconstructive surgery that gives them the use of their eyes, they have to learn to see. They don't just open up their eyes and see the world as a sighted person does. The brain needs to rewire in a multitude of ways, and that's a lot of work.

So much of what we learn about the brain comes from cases in which things go wrong or have been surgically altered. Oliver Sachs writes about a case in which brain damage in a woman affected only the visual cortex related to movement. The woman would see still shots. She couldn't cross the street because she couldn't see the car coming at her; it would just jump from one spot to another. Can you even imagine what life was like for her?

When you see objects moving, you're not really seeing an object that's moving, you're seeing an object that has "movement" and "direction" attached to it as qualities. There's a part of your brain that says, "I see these lines," there's another part of your visual cortex that says, "I see the color yellow," another part that says "I see the object there," and another that says, "I see that the object is moving in a certain direction." And then your brain combines all of these things into a speeding New York taxi-cab in the street.

It's tempting to think of vision as being like a giant movie screen on which the outside world is projected. Tempting, but totally incorrect. In fact, vision is more like an artist painting a picture of something that she cannot directly see. She pieces it together by knowing the general location, outline, whether or not it is moving, whether or not it's in color, and so on.

The visual process begins in the eye as light hitting the retina, stimulating light-sensitive cells (rods and cones), which, in turn, send signals back into the back of the brain towards the visual cortex, the occipital lobe. The signals are partly shunted to the amygdala, which makes a "quick and dirty" determination as to whether the stimulus is worthy of a fight or flight response (see Amygdala Hijack). Another portion of the signal carries on to the visual cortex, where it arrives at an area called V1.

V1 is the closest thing to the metaphorical movie screen that we find in the visual cortex. It essentially maps the signals coming in from the eye onto a distorted "fish-eye" screen in the visual cortex, point-to-point. The problem with the images on V1 is that they are spatially distorted, unclear, and do not have color or movement. In fact, if all we had was the V1 area of the visual cortex, we would hardly be able to see at all. Fortunately, V1 is not the end of the visual story.

Once the light reaches the visual cortex, it follows two

pathways. The first is the "What" pathway. The What pathway considers the size, shape, and color of the object seen. This information is then routed to higher brain centers that determine what kind of object it is, what specific object it is, and, ultimately, what the object "means."

The second pathway is known as the "Where" pathway. Signals going down the Where pathway are analyzed to determine the object's relative and absolute location and whether and how it is moving.

What we actually have is a bunch of photons hitting the eyes and signals being sent back to the visual cortex, which strives to make sense of it. And what an amazing job it does! More astonishing is the fact that all the different areas of the visual cortex don't actually "see" movement, colors, lines, depth, or all the features of vision, but vibration. Light and energy is bouncing throughout the visual cortex and being coded, rehashed, and re-created. Oh yeah, and it's being turned upside down and flipped over . . . whew! It's exhausting just to think about!

One third of the brain is taken up with constructing what you think you see. All that we actually see from our eyes is the vibration of light. As you look around your room right now, take a moment to appreciate what an amazing experience you're having. There is no other species on the planet that sees like humans do. There is no other species that is prepared to devote one pound of brain matter to constructing this amazing visual illusion that we call reality.

Since it's all being generated inside your head, you're never really here, *now*. This whole "Be here now" concept is, in reality, impossible. Everything happening *now* is experienced a fraction of a fraction of a fraction of a second late, being the time it takes your brain to do all the calisthenics to create a visual reality. Visual reality feels like a seamless construct, but it does take time . . . not a long time . . . not minutes or even seconds but fractions of a second so that, still, everything we're seeing now is actually the past.

How NLP Uses the What and Where Pathways

We mentioned earlier that each sensory system or modality has a collection of different qualities or distinctions called submodalities. Modern neuroscience shows the validity of this viewpoint in that vision, for example, is made up of different attributes, such as color, location, movement, depth, and so on, each stored in a different area of the visual cortex.

When we work with submodalities in NLP, we typically consider a particular object, or a particular scene, using the What pathway. We might then manipulate the information in the Where pathway in regard to location (for example, in a typical NLP Map Across"), or movement (for example, in the Swish pattern). Distance and objective position are determined using the visual areas V3 and V6, respectively, in the Where pathway.

Let's consider the Map Across and the Swish patterns in light of what we know about the visual cortex:

The Map Across

The Map Across works on the presupposition that the brain codes information according to submodalities. A principal submodality is position and other submodalities include:

- Size (which itself is a proxy for "distance"; i.e., position along a near-far axis: the closer an object is, the bigger it is; the farther away it is, the smaller it is).
- Brightness (again, this is a proxy for distance).
- Other submodalities, such as associated or dissociated, framed or unframed, still shot or movie, sound or no-

sound, and so on.

By using submodalities, particularly location, size, and brightness, we can check whether there are differences between two internal representations. For example, suppose we ask a client to think of something she is confident about versus something she is not that confident about. We then ask her to notice the different qualities of the associated pictures visualized; for example, "Where is the picture about confidence as opposed to the picture of lack of confidence?" "How close are the pictures?" "How bright are the pictures?" And so on.

After comparing the differences between the two pictures, we can help the client change the submodalities of the less confident picture into those of the more confident picture. If our presupposition is correct—that submodalities contain unconscious coding about the meaning of pictures (for example, whether a person feels confident or not), then we can become more confident about something simply by changing qualities, such as location, color, size and brightness, of the pictures associated with it.

We know that the visual cortex has different areas, and each area has a different function. Your brain is taking the separate pieces of visual experience from all the different areas and reconstructing them one by one, yet we have the experience of seeing the world in a nice cohesive way. The world seen is a neural fabrication, with your brain filling in gaps, making assumptions, filtering information unconsciously, and generally creating the world you *think* you see. And your episodic memories are stored in your visual cortex.

Given these two facts: 1) Memories are stored in the visual cortex and 2) The visual cortex stores individual pieces of information, such as whether something is moving or not, what color is it, and so on, it's obvious that your brain is going to code information in terms of those submodalities. How could it possibly do anything else? As hypnosis and NLP trainers, we love this fact.

Because memory is stored this way, according to various distinctions, specific pieces of coding can be changed, and this can change the whole way we experience memory. We can change the location or the color, whether it's moving or still, or any other feature of how we—and our clients—are experiencing a memory. We can learn how the client accesses confident memories and use this as a template as described above. This allows us to take imagined future moments, such as giving a talk (if the client has a fear of public speaking), and recode them in the submodalities of a confident memory.

This is the map-across technique of NLP. If you examine how the submodalities of a memory in which a client feels confident are compared with those of a memory in which she has no confidence, you will discover fundamental differences in how information is coded in at least one of the visual areas. It might be the visual area related to location; that is, where does the client see the confident picture inside her mind, and where does she see the not-confident picture? Then we take this element of the image and change the location of the not-confident picture to that of the confident picture.

Say a fellow wants to be able to cook. He's not confident in the kitchen, but he's fantastic at racing cars. When he thinks of cooking, the picture is here on the left in his mind, but when he think of racing cars, he sees it on his right. The two images are coded differently in the brain. The trick is to take the picture of cooking and move it to where the racing car picture is. Now, the brain thinks, "Oh, I am confident about cooking!" Switching the pictures has the effect of recoding on the lowest, most fundamental levels of the visual cortex. This particular section of the visual cortex—the one that maps location relative to a person—keeps confident things in one place and less confident things in another.

Once you know how the visual cortex works, submodalities and mapping across makes sense. It is how Melissa gets her taxes done, every year. No kidding. Because she's usually teaching a class in April, she'll use herself as an example when teaching this pattern:

"When I think about something I have to do but don't feel motivated to do, like taxes, I notice that the image of me with a mountain of receipts is down to my right, it's in black and white, and a still shot. The feeling in my body is kind of flat, and I can almost hear myself say *'ugh.'* Then, I think of something I never hesitate for, something I find absolutely motivating, like opening a new book from one of my favorite authors. That image is big and bright and front and center. The feeling in my body about that image has movement to it, and I think, *'Yes!'* to myself.

"So, I take this image of taxes and imagine sending it way off into the distance. Then, I imagine it, like a boomerang, slamming back into the position where the motivating image of the new book is. I see the image front and center, big and bright. It works. It's how I got my first book done. There are so many ways to play with this. With the taxes, since it's hard to get excited about it, I go for the end result. In other words, I see myself sealing the envelope and feel the feeling of 'whew, it's done!' I then use that to motivate me by attaching the feeling to the image slamming into the motivating location."

When Melissa used this pattern to write her first book, she kept focusing on the final word, the finished manuscript, and attached that feeling to the image of sitting at the desk and writing. She found that focusing on the emotion attached to the end result works to get motivated about most of the things that a person procrastinates about. We procrastinate because the task at hand, such as organizing closets or spring cleaning, is just not fun. But imagine, if you will, that your space is completely clean and organized or your book or taxes are done, and notice how this accomplishment feels. That's energy worth mining! By adding the emotion attached to the completion of the task, we are anchoring it to the behavior and stimulating long-term potentiation. It's Hebb's Law of firing and wiring once again.

And we're doing this work in the working memory, not the visual cortex because, in order to do the work, it has to be brought into working memory. How do we keep what we're doing in working memory? Dopamine! It has to be fun, interesting, and engaging! It's the theatre of change work that keeps the client's attention. Clients need the attention and emotional impact to reconsolidate the memory. Patterns like this are dopamine-laced because they are fascinating and the effects are felt immediately!

This is how the visual cortex works. Remember, different parts are responsible for different aspects of what we see.

The Swish

The swish pattern technique uses a brain area of the Where path, specifically, the V5, or movement portion, of the visual cortex. In the Swish pattern, we move a picture of something that we wish to change into the distance and then bring it back as a new picture.

The Swish also utilizes the fact that the brain codes things differently depending on whether they are within or out of reach. We discuss this concept more fully in Chapter 10, the chapter on space and movement. Think of a child who has not yet learned to walk who is deciding whether to put her attention on something that is near and easy to grasp or out of reach. Objects that are within reach feel more immediate and cultivate more attention density.

When we do the Swish pattern, we take an object, typically one that creates a compulsive feeling for clients, such as a cigarette or a problem food, and move it from being close up to being far away. We move it from being in reach to out of reach. We simultaneously ask the clients to move a picture of their ideal self from faraway to close enough to touch.

Demo of the Swish Pattern

For those unfamiliar with the Swish pattern, the following demo is an abbreviated version from Shawn's book The Swish Pattern: An In-Depth Look at this Powerful NLP Pattern [New York: Changing Minds Publishing. 2013].

Coach: So, Janet, you want to become a non-smoker?

Janet: Yes.

Coach: And why do you want to make this change?

Janet: It just annoys me that cigarettes have this hold over me. I have control over other areas of my life, but the cigarettes seem to have control over me. I don't like it.

Coach: I wouldn't like that either. I'm sure you want to feel in control of what you put inside yourself. I see that you brought your cigarettes along . . . What brand are they?

Janet: Marlboro.

Coach: Is that the brand that you normally smoke?

Janet: Yes.

Coach: Can you tell me about the times and places when you typically smoke over the course of the day?

Janet: Yes, I smoke first thing in the morning with my first coffee, then at work when I get bored. I have a cigarette at lunchtime and usually after dinner.

Coach: So, let's take one of those occasions. Let's take the cigarette that you have in the morning. Where are you when you smoke that?

Janet: On my front porch.

Coach: So you're on your front porch. Why do you smoke then?

Janet: I guess it wakes me up.

Coach: And as you are on your front porch, what do you see immediately before you smoke?

Janet: I can see my cigarettes, the pack.

Coach: So, you see the pack of cigarettes, and you feel it is time to smoke. So, what I would like you to do is pick up your packet of cigarettes. As you look at the packet of cigarettes, what do you notice about the pack? What catches your attention about the design?

Janet: I notice the gold foil on the front of the pack.

Coach: You notice the gold foil on the pack. And as you look at the gold foil on the pack, I would like you to pick someplace within that gold foil on the pack.

Janet: The lion and the unicorn. They have a shield between them. That's what catches my attention.

Coach: Okay, so, put the pack down for now. Now tell me again, why do you want to quit?

Janet: Because I feel awful. I just want to be free of the cigarettes.

Coach: And when you are living free of the cigarettes, living free as a healthy non-smoker, how will you be then as a person?

Janet: I won't have to hide my cigarettes! I'll be able to breathe easily. Actually, I've been thinking of running a marathon so I guess I'll be a marathon runner!

Coach: You'll be free and you'll be able to breathe easily. You'll be running a marathon! So, Janet, what I would like you to do now is to make the picture of yourself being free. If you could see yourself living free and breathing easily as a healthy non-smoker what would that be like?

Janet: I see myself running in a marathon!

Coach: You see yourself running in a marathon! And when you see yourself running in a marathon, when you look at yourself, what lets you know that you're free and that you can breathe easily as a healthy non-smoker?

Janet: I look healthy and strong, and I'm smiling!

Coach: So, let's take that picture of you in the marathon, looking healthy and strong and smiling. I'd like you to take that picture and make it very small and embed it in the middle of the shield between the lion and the unicorn on the pack of cigarettes, right there. Can you do that for me?

Janet: Yes.

Coach: So, in a moment—but not yet—I'm going to ask you to do the following: I'm going to ask you to look at the cigarettes and notice the gold foil and the lion and the unicorn and the shield between them. Notice that in the center of the shield is that small picture of you looking healthy and strong and smiling, running in the marathon. And when I tell you—but not before—I want you to imagine that picture of you, healthy and strong and smiling, running in the marathon, getting very big, life-size, bigger than life, so it totally covers the pack of cigarettes. Got it? The picture of you, healthy and strong and smiling, running in the marathon, just bursting out of the shield.

Okay, we are going to do that again. First, blank the screen. Now, see that pack of cigarettes, see the lion and the unicorn with a shield in between them, and see that tiny picture of you, healthy and strong and smiling, in the center of the shield. Now—1, 2, 3—the picture of you, strong and healthy and smiling, bursting out. Now blank the screen. One more time— 1, 2, 3—the picture of you, strong and healthy and smiling, right there in front of you.

How was that?

Janet: That was amazing!

Coach: Pick up your pack of cigarettes. Take one out.

[The client picks up the pack and opens it. Her hand reaches for a cigarette and then she stops.]

Janet: I feel my. . . my feelings for them have changed, I don't . . .

We hope you are beginning to see the power of having a clear view of the visual cortex, and how this can paint a compelling picture of the future for your client!

Chapter 7: Neurotransmitters (Bad Dopamine)

In this chapter, we are going to tell you about a couple of common neurotransmitters and how they can create problems and help with solutions.

Before we get started we should be clear about what a neurotransmitter is. We, the authors, don't know about you, but when we think about the brain, the picture that comes to mind is a network of wires (neurons) that pass, or don't pass, electrical signals to one another, meaning that they either fire or not. While this is not a bad picture to have, it misses several elements of how the brain actually works. One of these elements is that the signals themselves are not just electrical on-off pulses, but are actually sophisticated chemical messengers in their own right. These chemical messengers are called neurotransmitters. They are released from a neuron and travel across a gap, known as the synaptic cleft, to a neuroreceptor in a neighboring neuron.

Neurotransmitters were discovered in 1921 by Otto Loewi (1873-1961).

We normally wouldn't bother providing you with trivia like this except that the story of his discovery is quite fascinating, and was actually used as the basis of an episode of one of our favorite philosophers, Jerry Seinfeld. You see, our hero Otto actually dreamed about an experiment for discovering neurotransmitters. The dream involved two frogs. After having the dream in the middle of the night, Otto woke up, scribbled his thoughts down on a scrap of paper, and went back to sleep. If you are familiar with the related Jerry Seinfeld episode, you may remember the same thing happened to Jerry, although in Jerry's case, he dreamed a joke. Otto and years later, Jerry both awoke in the morning to discover neither could read his own scrawled handwriting.

Fortunately for neuroscience, Otto's unconscious mind provided him with a rerun of the dream during which he remembered the experiment and carried it out the next day, thereby discovering neurotransmitters (Seinfeld is also able to remember the joke during his reruns, although as it turns out, it just wasn't funny). We won't tell you what Otto's experiment was, as it ended badly for the two frogs involved.

So what do neurotransmitters actually do? Each neurotransmitter is emitted by one neuron, called the presynaptic neuron. It floats across the synaptic cleft and is received by the next neuron, called the postsynaptic neuron.

Each separate neurotransmitter sends a very different message. One might say, "I'm thirsty. Put the tea on" and another, "Are you sure you turned off the gas?" We're joking; they don't say things like that, but they do trigger specific responses through specific pathways that result in specific feelings, such as desire for a cup of tea or worry that you left the gas on after you made the tea.

The two main neurotransmitters that do almost 80% of the firing are in charge of revving up or calming down the system.

Glutamate excites the system and stirs activity. When we talked about Hebb's Law, we discussed how neurons fire together, creating a sensitivity for the next firing. This sensitivity is primed by glutamate. Glutamate gets the neurons excited enough to make friends and connections and comes into play in almost every piece of change work we do. The other half of the equation, as far as our sessions go, is GABA, which is short for, gamma-aminobutyric acid. (Try saying that five times fast!) This neurotransmitter is released when we do exercises to relax and calm down the system. It is the stuff of anti-anxiety medication, such as the benzodiazepine marketed as Valium. Glutamate and GABA do most of the work in regulating the nervous system, but there are more than 60 other neurotransmitters playing different roles in the brain.

This book isn't the place for an exhaustive discussion of all of these neurotransmitters so let's just focus on the main three that regulate mood. The three main neuromodulators that regulate mood are serotonin, norepinephrine, and our old pal, dopamine. Most people are familiar with serotonin because of popular, and arguably overly-prescribed, drugs such as Prozac. Serotonin controls emotional tone and reactivity. Many of the techniques in this book that help to neutralize negative reactions and inspire positive emotions help in the creation and release of serotonin.

Norepinephrine activates attention by amplifying the signals involved in motivation and arousal. It plays a big role, along with dopamine, in creating attention density, a topic we discussed at length because of its importance in creating lasting changes.

Because most of the changes people come to us for involve attention, learning, movement, memory, pleasure, and addiction, we will spend the rest of this chapter discussing dopamine.

The Dopamine Circuit

Dopamine is mainly concerned with the reward circuit. This sounds pretty good, and, most of the time, it is. But sometimes dopamine gets a bit carried away with its job, and then things can go awry.

The "reward circuit" runs along the mesolimbic and mesocortical pathways, beginning in the ventral tegmental area (VTA) and running to the nucleus accumbens as well the PFC. There is no reason you need to know this to understand the role dopamine plays in creating problems and solutions, but some people are fact junkies who get a dopamine rush out of neuroscience trivia. In translating this into English, it means that your brain is wired to reward you with pleasure for taking certain actions, and not necessarily the actions that are best for you!

Neurotransmitters in the reward circuit—dopamine in particular—can create feelings of pleasure in many parts of the brain, the so-called dopamine rush. But what is unusual about dopamine is that it is not just released when something pleasant happens but also when a decision is made to undertake an action that the brain perceives as pleasant. This means that dopamine is designed to reward actions that have a chance of success, and it rewards taking these actions even if the actions actually fail. The reward circuit does not reward us only for achieving worthwhile goals, but also for taking actions toward those goals.

This rewarding of actions that could lead to achieving a goal is an excellent evolutionary development because it helps to motivate us to move towards things, such as food for survival and sex for reproduction, even though we have no guarantee that we will get them. Unfortunately, this aspect of dopamine can be damaging in the 21st century when we're not spending our time chasing food or a mate. Well, not all of our time, anyway. Instead, people may be engaged in activities that are less constructive, such as buying a Lotto ticket because it provides the chance of becoming a millionaire. Buying the ticket, therefore, creates a wonderful dopamine rush in spite of the fact that the chance of winning is about the same as finding a cab in New York that will take you to the Bronx at 5 PM on a rainy Friday evening.

But here is the problem; the Lotto-addict gets a dopamine rush from buying a Lotto ticket because it comes with an expectation of reward. If this person is one of the 99.9% of people who don't win the jackpot, then there is a dopamine crash. A dopamine crash is when the level of dopamine in the brain suddenly goes down, triggered by the result of an action not being what was hoped for. The dopamine crash can feel so bad that the addict has to run out and buy another Lotto-ticket to try to maintain the dopamine high. [Volow ND, et al. Addiction: beyond dopamine reward circuitry. *Proceedings of the National Academy of Sciences U S A*. 2011;108(37):15037-42.

When you consider that other activities that can create a dopamine rush include using recreational drugs, smoking, drinking, eating, gambling, surfing the Internet, and other compulsions, you can begin to understand why dopamine can create problems when triggered in the wrong context. In this case, the dopamine rewards the activity even though the final outcome is negative: losing all your money in Las Vegas, for example! So, the addict continues the addiction, irrespective of whether he or she wins or loses. The teenager who spends all free time on the Internet becomes addicted to the activity irrespective of the impact on other aspects of life.

Application to Coaching

When Shawn is in a restaurant, he will slowly peruse the list of desserts, imagining each treat appearing before him in all its glory. He savors the imagined taste of each dessert and revels in the thought of the creamy crunchy texture of each item as he imagines its sugary sweetness descending to his stomach. By the end of the process, he is thoroughly sick of sweets and sends the waitress away when she comes to take the dessert order!

It can be useful to know, in a coaching context, that the addiction or compulsion very often is to the activity, not necessarily the results of the activity. By savoring the possibility of engaging in the activity mentally, a person can still get the dopamine hit and skip the negative ramifications of the actual behavior!

Dopamine and Learning

As we already discussed, dopamine is essential for attention density and learning. One of the main reasons we have dopamine and a pleasure circuit inside our brains is to learn new and useful behaviors. Because we evolved by paying attention to things that cause us fear or pleasure, the brain doses us with dopamine when we feel these strong responses.

We also have explained how dopamine alerts another brain area, the hippocampus, that there is something worth learning. The hippocampus responds by taking the experience that resulted in the reward, whether the external environment or the contents of working memory, and encoding it into long-term memory. The result: we learn.

If you want to learn something consciously, you have to pay attention. The problem is, we are biologically wired to be listening for threats. Distractions will snatch attention away, because the brain doesn't want you to be snatched away by a tiger. The fire engines outside and the noise down the hall are some of the distractions that your brain is listening for in case those things suggest approaching danger. However, it's also very important that we pay attention if we want to learn something. Our brain pays attention thanks to our old friend dopamine.

We've described the gate that stands between what you're paying attention to and the rest of the world with all of its distractions and how dopamine closes that gate and keeps the distractions out so we go into a learning trance of focus. Dopamine is a reward, saying, "This activity is good so pay attention because you want to learn it."

That's why dopamine locks the attention on one thing, and blocks out everything else. If anyone has ever tried to get a child's attention when she is playing a video game, you'll know just how strong that gate can be! Or how about when someone says something while you're watching your favorite TV show, and you don't even hear the person. Dopamine is locking your attention in and blocking other stimuli.

As an aside, dopamine actually locks attention in an "inverted U" pattern, meaning the more dopamine you have, the more attention you pay to what is going on, and the more you learn., but if too much dopamine is released, concentration and attention actually decrease . . . so don't have too much fun!

The Brain's Addiction to the Problem

There's also the dark side to the reward system for problems. These are not usually thought of as being addictions, but in many ways they are.

The brain and body can literally become addicted to a problem. Many addictive drugs work by altering the level of or the sensitivity to transmitters such as serotonin and dopamine. When the levels of transmitters are altered in this way over a period of time, tolerance and addiction can develop. Tolerance develops in the addict, who needs more and more of the drug in order to feel the high the drug provides because, when the neuroreceptors in the brain that receive the neurotransmitters are overexposed, they can become less sensitive, and, hence, larger amounts are required to get the same effect.

Any emotion that you habitually feel creates a set of neurotransmitters that bind to the receptors on the cells so that a tolerance to the emotion is created. The neurons generate more receptors to the neurotransmitters of that emotion so that the emotion has to get stronger and generate more neurotransmitters to get the same effect. In the same way that heroine binds with the opiate receptors, stress and all emotions have the same binding mechanism and become addictions as well. The brain can behave like the addict, needing more and more stress and becoming uncomfortable when the stress is not available so much so, that the brain can generate signals that tell a person that she should be stressed.

Dr. Schwartz and Deceptive Brain Messages

Because of the brain's addiction to a problem, the brain may give a person reasons to maintain the problem, to be stressed or depressed or whatever, including telling the person that whatever she does to relieve the stress really doesn't work!

Dr. Schwartz talks about this effect at length, referring to it as Deceptive Brain Messages. Dr. Schwartz defines a deceptive brain message as "any false . . . thought or unhelpful impulse . . . that takes you away from your true goals . . . i.e., your true self."

Examples of deceptive brain messages might include:

- "I'll just have one more cigarette; I'll quit tomorrow."
- "Why am I such a failure? I'll never be able to do this."
- "Why do I always feel this way?"
- "It's been such a tough day; I deserve a drink!"

The concept of deceptive brain messages, as laid out by Dr. Schwartz, is based on the premise that whenever a person does something repeatedly, the brain and body learn to expect this behavior. They become "addicted" to this behavior and to the state of mind and body that goes along with it. This addiction leads the mind-body to do whatever is necessary to maintain the state, including generating thoughts, impulses, urges and desires that force, trick, or persuade a person to continue the behavior.

Schwartz speculates that these deceptive brain messages give rise to uncomfortable physical or emotional sensations, such as cravings, which are relieved by unhealthy responses. However, the relief is temporary, and the deceptive brain messages return. Ultimately, the negative behaviors can become intertwined with the person's identity; for example: "I am a smoker."

When we are doing change work with a client, it is quite possible that the client's mind-body is conspiring against us— and against the client—to maintain the current problem. In this sense, as Dr. Schwartz says, the problem itself becomes addictive.

This suggests that some positive steps can be taken to deal with deceptive brain messages. For example, the change worker can do a pre-frame whereby the client is made aware of the possibility that deceptive brain messages may arise in the future and that, if they do, it is simply a sign that change has happened and that the mind-body is getting used to the new state. This is the basis of Dr. Schwartz's work.

We can also bring the change to the attention of the client's conscious mind so that the conscious mind knows—is convinced—that change has happened. Later, deceptive brain messages such as "That didn't work" may then be neutralized before they arise. One example of this is John Overdurf's reinforcement loop: "You changed? . . . How do you know? . . .

Are you sure? . . . Really? . . . How do you know? . . ." You are aiming for the client to be convincing the coach that she has changed, not the coach trying to convince the client!

Hope and Expectation

Ultimately, the victim of the deceptive brain messages realizes that there is a problem and wants things to be different. The question then arises as to why it is often so difficult to change?

One explanation is offered in the research of Donald Price, of the University of Florida. Dr. Price found that the desire to feel better is actually negatively correlated with feeling better; i.e.; the more a person wants to change, the harder change becomes. In fact it is the expectation of change that is most important to the outcome, not the desire for change. People are more likely to change if they expect to change, but not if they simply want to change. People can actually feel worse if they have low expectations of change but have high desires to avoid the negative outcome.

Now, it is very typical for a client to walk into the office with a high desire to avoid the problem and with low expectations of being able to change because she has lived with the problem for such a long time. So, although the problem is unpleasant, it also appears insoluble. Based on the research of Dr. Price, this is the worst possible position for the client to be in! Instead, we want to move the client to a position in which she is not focusing on avoiding the problem and has a high expectation of changing.

This is where sharing the ideas and examples from neuroscience really make a difference. By explaining to clients how they can rewire their brains or how, by changing the emotional content of a memory, unconscious reactions are influenced, you're setting an expectation for change. By using examples of other clients or research to support your claims, you are setting up a very different frame than the one that your clients have been using.

Dr. Schwartz's Brain Map

The resistance to change is caused by dopamine—the dark side of dopamine—and other neurotransmitters in the reward circuit. In his map of the mind, Dr. Schwartz essentially says that something happens in the world around us and that there is a part of the PFC that takes everything personally: "Why does this always happen to me! Nobody understands me! Everything is stressing me out!"

To relieve this stress, we have to go and do something. Maybe some retail therapy will help so we think, "I know, I'll go shopping. That'll make me feel better!" As soon as we decide that, the bad dopamine comes out and makes us feel good about shopping: "I'm going to go and buy a new pair of shoes!" Then, we might say, "Okay, that's good, but . . . I don't know, it wasn't as good as I thought it would be . . . " So, then, we have to go buy something else: "Oh, there's a Barnes and Noble over there. Let me go buy a book. That will definitely make me feel better!"

This is the loop. It's the bad dopamine that's making us feel good about the activity of shopping, but each time we buy something, it doesn't quite feel good enough. How many of us have gone out and bought a piece of clothing, put it in the closet, and never worn it. The activity is what the dopamine is rewarding us for, not necessarily the outcome.

According to Dr. Schwartz, this is the case with OCD sufferers. They get stressed and they think, "What can I do? I know. I'll go check all the windows!" And they get a dopamine rush. As they're checking the windows, they feel better, but when they sit down they realize that doing so wasn't that rewarding, but that's the only pattern that bad dopamine rewards them for so they think, "Well, that didn't do much good. I still feel like something is wrong so let me go check the windows again!" And then, they feel a compulsion to check the windows even though, consciously, they know the windows are locked.

It's an error-detection circuit, but it also includes a circuit that's connected to the gut. As we've discussed, Dr. Schwartz calls it the Uh-Oh Center. A person gets the sense that something is wrong, and this sensing is physically felt in the gut. If you have worked with an affected client, you'll see a visceral reaction. The reaction is not just an idea about having to wash the hands; it's a feeling, a drive. It feels like something is really wrong, and the only way to stop the stress is to give into an urge: check the window or wash the hands. And it is a dopamine hit, but it's temporary and fleeting, leading a person to repeat the behavior.

What happens when you decide to make a change in your life? "I'm not going to do this anymore. I don't need retail therapy; I have enough shoes. So, I'm going to change things!" Well, your body and brain are literally addicted to what you've been doing, and they experience withdrawal symptoms. Like junkies, they want to get back to where they were. Your mind and body want to get back to buying shoes so they're going to do anything they have to do to make you go out and shop.

Because the brain is addicted, it's going to say things such as, "This is not working. You know, you don't need to do this right now. You can make this change next week . . . ." The brain is going to think thoughts that lead to maintaining the problem behavior. And you are going to think that you are hearing yourself talking, but it isn't you; it's just your brain seeking to maintain the problem because it's addicted to it.

So, be aware that your client is going to leave your office and start to have thoughts: "Could it really be as easy as that? You've tried to change before and it never worked out. Why am I even bothering? I'm seeing my friends on the weekend, and they all smoke . . . maybe I'll wait until next week." All these brain messages are deceptive.

Dr. Schwartz, in his four-step process, is reframing these deceptive brain messages. When the brain says, "You don't need to quit now; you can do it next week." A person trained in the four-step process says, "Oy! I heard that! Shut up and go away!" That's step one. Then, the person says, "That's not me; that's my deceptive brain message." That's step two. Then, "I'm not going to smoke that cigarette; I'm going to do some bilateral stimulation." That's step three. Then, the person realizes, "Doing bilateral stimulation is better than smoking!" Step four.

In using the four-step process, you're pre-framing your client to expect that deceptive thoughts may arise and giving her this pre-set label: "Deceptive brain messages." This is a powerful metaphor to pre-arm your client against the thoughts and feeling that are going to later arise to try to take her back to old behavior. The reason someone gambles is because gambling provides a dopamine rush. It makes the person feel good. The person has a problem, such as being stressed at work, and the thought emerges: "I can't believe my boss, my client, all this shit. I'm going to Vegas!" But although the antidote to the stress—to gamble—provides a dopamine rush, it is only a temporary respite. After the behavior is repeated a few times and the body gets used to the dopamine rush, the person ups the game, ups the ante, literally.

When people make the decision to quit gambling because their relationship is falling apart or they've run out of money or they are in debt to "Little Jimmy" who is seven feet tall and carries a baseball bat around with him, their brains and bodies are still going to rebel against their better judgment. The brain is going to send whatever message it needs to send to get a person to go down to Vegas because that person's brain is addicted to the chemical related to the compulsion to gamble. The person's brain is going to say, "You know, you don't need to quit now. There's a big Billy Joel concert in Vegas now. You can quit after that!" Or it'll say, "You've never been able to quit. There's no chance. Don't even bother" or even, "Little Jimmy ain't so big . . . ."

After doing change work, we can say, "You've already changed, but because you're addicted to this behavior, your brain may try to make you do it. These are deceptive brain messages. These are lies that your brain is telling you because it wants you to go back to the problem." We always give clients recovery strategies and have them rehearse the strategies in case they should start to feel that the old pattern is kicking up. Teaching clients about deceptive brain messages helps with that.

The reward is the dopamine, which is related to the action of doing, or even thinking about doing the action so having clients mentally rehearse positive scenarios using multisensory visualizations gets more areas of the brain activated and starts to change the loop. It's the thought that's driving the force, not the action. It's the thought of wanting to wash the hands that has the most energy behind it, not the actual washing.

Neural-Darwinism

There's a concept called Neural-Darwinism that says that neurons in your brain compete for survival. To survive, the neuron strives to be part of a successful neural network, one that's active and fires often. Just like teenagers who want to be in some popular clique or group on Facebook, neurons want to be part of an active neural social network.

Neurons in a circuit responsible for smoking or that engage in retail therapy like being part of that network and will fight to survive. They're going to work against changing that habit so we need to understand how these neurons work to understand how to get them to do something more useful in order to rewire the brain.

When you understand how this works and how to reinforce new neural networks, you will be able to make it so that neurons that are no longer linked and being utilized for smoking, or any other habit, will either make different connections (which they usually do) or just be pruned away.

Loss and Mourning

Research tells us that the brain of a person who is grieving beyond the normal time scale is behaving in the same way as someone who is addicted, with the activation of the reward circuits discussed above [O'Connor MF, et al. Craving Love? Enduring grief activates the brain's reward center. *Neuroimage*. 2008;42(2):969-72.]

So, the grief is an addiction in that it becomes a habituated dopamine hit. It's also an over-activation of the right hemisphere, which has more global tendencies. Because of this, the grieving person is more likely to hear universal quantifiers (words such as "always" or "never"), such as, "It's always like this; nothing will ever turn out right." With repetition, that neural network gets reinforced over and over and over again.

Conclusion

Dopamine rewards you. It doesn't reward you for getting things right. It rewards you for the act of going after things, irrespective of the result. When you get the outcome, your brain then tests it: "Is the outcome as good as I thought it was going to be." If it is, it maintains the level of dopamine. If it's not, the level of dopamine drops. For gamblers, it's the betting that produces the hit; even losing can maintain the level of dopamine as long as the gambler can bet again. As soon as the gambler wins, that person may realize it's not a big deal and the gambler's level of dopamine drops.

Chapter 8: The Emotional Brain

We are all on drugs. In many ways, we are high or stoned on emotions. We can get hooked on specific ones and feel withdrawal as strongly as from any external substance. Research shows that people who lack emotions because they have suffered damage to some part of the brain aren't able to function in the world. They lose their drive and can no longer set and move towards even the simplest of goals.

Change work is all about emotions, reducing some, and cultivating others. When our clients can connect with the right emotional state in the right context, their problems can be solved.

The Amygdala

The amygdala is a part of the limbic system and is responsible for "primary," or primitive, emotions such as fear and anger. Sensory information coming into the brain is ultimately routed to the higher processing areas, such as the PFC, for more sophisticated analysis. However, the information is also sent, for a more immediate response, through a much shorter route to the amygdala. These pathways are sometimes referred to as the "high road" to the PFC, and the "low road" to the amygdala. The amygdala does a "quick and dirty" check of the sensory information to see if it poses a potential threat. If so, the amygdala immediately prepares the body for a "fight or flight" response.

Just imagine you're walking through the woods at night and you see a long snakey thing on the path. The image goes to your eyes, then to your visual cortex, and on to your PFC. This is the high road, or the slow road. So the frontal brain thinks, "Hmm, I'm not sure what that is. Is it a snake or just a stick?" But the picture also goes to the amygdala by the low road, which is a lot faster. The amygdala checks the object against its limited database of potential threats, and thinks, "That could be a snake!" It immediately prepares the body to run:.; you feel your heart begin to race, your vision focuses in on the object, and you begin to back up even though you're not yet sure what the object is.

A fraction of a second later, the image of the possible snake gets to the visual cortex, comes to the front of the brain, and your PFC says, "It's just a stick." And you go, "Phew." This is how it's supposed to work. You see the object, the amygdala puts you into a state in which, if it *is* a snake, you're ready for action. You're good to go either way because you're immediately in fight or flight mode. Then, the front of your brain says, "It's just a stick." The PFC sends the appropriate message to the amygdala, and the "all-clear" signal is sounded.

We owe our evolution to the freeze, fight, or flight response. Most people think of the stress response as the fight or flight response, but the first response to threat is usually to freeze. When confronting danger, most of us stop first. Think about a lizard or rabbit or something that's being threatened. The creature freezes. Sometimes our clients show us this freeze response when they associate into their issue. When we see this, we get them to move their bodies. Some practitioners of somatic experiencing will get clients to shake it off in the same

171

way animals in the wild process through the freeze response.

So, the amygdala is a very important part of the limbic system. The limbic system is a set of structures in the brain that govern emotion, behavior, motivation, and long-term memory, as well as our sense of smell. Your limbic system connects to the brain stem, which controls our basic functions, such as heartbeat and so on. Above this lies the neocortex, governing all higher cognitive functions. When things are functioning really well, everything is integrated, but sometimes, things get stuck in the limbic system, and the connection with the PFC—the executive brain—is lost.

When we help our clients to put words or a narrative to their fears, we help link the unwarranted fears to the PFC. Change work is all about reintegrating communication between lower and higher brain function. When someone has irrational or unwarranted fears, the top-down processing using the PFC isn't working; the higher and lower brain systems are not connecting. The human part of the brain is saying, "Look, it's not a big deal" but the amygdala doesn't listen because it's too busy going "Aaaarrrggghhhhhh!"

The Hippocampus and Stress

The hippocampus registers memories of danger and trauma so when it gets too flooded in one direction, it no longer functions properly. It overcompensates. Research shows that, with chronic stress, something like 20% of the hippocampus begins to disintegrate. It literally shrinks [Bremner JD. Does stress damage the brain? *Biological Psychiatry*. 1999;45(7):797-805.]

When the amygdala begins to experience the fight or flight response on a regular basis, it becomes overly sensitive. Between the hippocampus overcompensating and the amygdala overreacting, the stress responses start to generalize out so that what might have started as a fear of speaking in public, generalizes to fear of groups, then fear of any social interaction. It's amazing how fast the brain can learn and generalize fears across contexts.

Ironically, generalization is the key process behind creating generative changes with our clients. When doing the meta pattern, the client is asked to think of other instances in which she would like to feel confident (for example), and then confidence is conditioned into behavior associated with specific situations until the brain thinks, "Ok, I got it, 'feel confident.'" The brain is a pattern-making, generalizing machine. In helping it along, the very thing that created the problem can be used to generate the solution.

The brain doesn't just learn not to be afraid or angry or upset about a specific issue, it learns that it can learn. It learns that it can change. It uses one small example of change and then another and makes a generalization from that. If you try to change everything at once, you're aiming for a circuit in the brain that's too big. That's why we ask a client during change work, "Tell me about one specific time and place," so the circuit we are working with becomes very small and easier to change. If a client is afraid of flying and is also afraid of mice . . . and elevators . . . a change work practitioner would just help her with her most pressing issue. Even the fear of flying is too big, so start with a particular memory of a particular flight, or even one particular moment in one particular flight.

When we link the resource into that smaller network, it still gets linked into everywhere else because the networks are all connected, but the resource is less likely to become overwhelmed. If fear of flying is the issue, after we've addressed one specific flight, we then work on another flight. Then, we do another flight until the client says, "You know? I can't seem to find that fear of flying. I feel fine about flying now." And so you address another issue and say something like, "Okay then, tell me about mice, about one particular memory with a mouse that you experienced." Then, you deal with that mouse, and then you deal with another mouse until the client says, "You know what? I'm not afraid of mice anymore." And in the next session you say, "Let's deal with elevators" and the client replies, "Strange you should say that; I took the elevator to get here and wasn't afraid at all. I'm not sure how that happened!" But it did, because the client's brain has learned how to learn. More importantly, it has learned how not to be afraid.

Sometimes, the amygdala reacts so strongly that a subsequent signal from the PFC that everything is safe gets lost. The danger signals from the amygdala continue to be sent to the body, which reacts accordingly. This is known as the amygdala hijack because the amygdala hijacks the rest of the nervous system. This is the basis of phobias and similar strong fears and reactions to things that are probably not dangerous.

The amygdala hijack can be dealt with using techniques such as the NLP V-K dissociation pattern (the "phobia cure"). This pattern uses various submodality shifts to allow a client to see or imagine seeing the object that would normally cause the negative response but see it in such a way that the amygdala does not trigger the reaction.

The classic V-K dissociation uses metaphors involving comfort and safety, such as watching the stimulus on a movie screen. It also changes a number of submodalities to change the coding, for example, by seeing the stimulus in black-and-white, abnormally small, far away, or playing the movie of the stimulus backwards, with no sound, or with a comical soundtrack.

Experiencing the stimulus with some combination of these submodality shifts is likely to rob the experience of its negative emotional attachments so that the client imagines seeing the stimulus (e.g., the snake), without feeling the response. As we discussed in the section on reconsolidation and memory

174

extinction, this will ultimately remove the previous phobic response from the memory. The amygdala has been retrained.

Client Example of the V-K Pattern

Client: Ever since I was on a plane that had this terrible turbulence, I have this fear of flying. It was years ago, but when I even think about getting on a plane, I remember that scene and I start to panic . . .

Coach: Stop. Let's make an old movie of this event. The movie will start and end with you feeling safe. Ok? In other words, there was the time before you got on the plane where you were safe. And when you landed and got off the plane you are safe. Right?
So, the movie's opening scene is you at the gate, safe, about to board, and the movie ends with the plane safely landing and you leaving the airport. Got it?

Client: I think so.

Coach: Good. So, take a moment to close your eyes, and remember how you feel when you are at your most comfortable, and take a few relaxing breaths, knowing you're safe. Where are you the most comfortable?

Client: Sitting in my easy chair, with my cat, just watching TV. Just petting her and feeling relaxed.

Coach: Now, as you're imagining sitting in the chair, comfortable, feeling the calm of your cat, imagine you can see, on your TV, an old grainy black and white still shot—like it's on pause—the ending scene of that movie, where you're already out of the airport and safe. Can you imagine that?

Client: Yes. Just a paused black and white image of myself?

Coach: Yes. And back up as if you can take a perspective from behind your chair. Now imagine you can see yourself in that chair, comfortable, petting your cat and watching the TV, with you with the image of you on it. Can you do that?

Client: Yes.

Coach: Good. When you're ready, imagine you have the remote, and I want you to rewind that old movie so you see yourself watching it on the TV, going backwards very quickly through that flight so you end at the beginning scene before you get on the plane, and you're safe. Got it? Now rewind it fast . . . and pause. You're safe.

Client: That was kind of funny, watching me in the chair watching the movie go backward.

Coach: Yep. And we can make it even funnier. Do you know any good circus music? In a moment, you will watch that movie, in fast forward, grainy black and white, but add circus music so you see yourself jostling around in that turbulence, but it's to circus music, and fast forward. Got it? Ready and press play . . . [Coach hums circus music.] And pause the last scene where you're safe.

Now, in a moment, I want you to imagine floating into the TV, into that paused moment, so that you can rewind the movie with you in it. You will see, hear, and feel everything going in fast rewind, even the circus music. And ready, go. . . and pause at the beginning, and you're safe. Now, float back into your easy chair and imagine petting your cat. How do you feel now?

Client: Strange. But comfortable.

Coach: Good. I'm strange. And comfortable too.

Client: [Laughing.] I won't argue that.

Coach: And as you're laughing, watch that old movie playing, [coach hums circus music] and pause when you're safe.

Client: The movie seems to be getting sillier and sillier. I see my panic-face, but it's like an act. Bad acting . . .

Coach: I say, blame the director . . . but before we do, imagine floating into the movie that's still paused at the end and press rewind so you are a part of the silly action, in reverse . . . everything going backward . . . and pause at the beginning when you're safe.

Client: [Laughing.] Were you humming the circus music backward?

Coach: Trying to . . . and I'm curious to know what happens when you think of that memory of that flight . . .

Client: Well, it just feels like a silly movie with bad acting . . . I can't quite feel the fear I had. It must have been the circus music. . .

Coach: Probably. And as you imagine having to get on a plane tomorrow, what are you noticing?

Client: Uh . . . I don't know. I can't really connect to it . . .

Coach: And how do you want to feel?

Client: Calm, relaxed, maybe even excited to be going on a trip . . .

Coach: And when you imagine your cat on your lap and you feel calm and relaxed, where in your body do you feel that calm?

Client: In my arms, my chest. I just feel a general sense of relaxation.

Coach: And as you feel this now, imagine getting on that plane and sitting easy in the chair. How do you feel now?

Client: Ok. I feel calm, which is strange . . .

Coach: As you are . . . feeling calm, relaxed, sitting in the chair as the plane takes off. How do you feel now?

Client: Calm, still. I'm even imagining looking out the window . . . I feel ok. How did you do that?

Coach: Don't blame me. It's your show. Now, imagine there's even a bit of turbulence, as sometimes happen. How do you feel now?

Client: It's so weird. I started to feel a little anxious, but then I pictured my face as it looked silly in the movie, and it seems like bad acting.

Coach: That's right. And when you know that, and you can relax, imagining now being on a plane, how do you feel?

Client: Relaxed.

Coach: And if you were to try to get that old feeling back . . . what happens?

Client: I can't. It doesn't feel real. It feels like acting.

Coach: And that's a rap.

In the above example, we start by interrupting the client as soon as she starts to associate into the problem. By saying, "Stop!" and then delivering a set of slightly confusing directions for the movie, we dissociate (step two of the meta pattern). The coach is also priming with the constant embedded command of "you're safe."

We then ask about a comfortable state that the client can associate into (step three in the meta pattern). In the example, we use the chair that the client mentioned (instead of the typical movie theater scenario) to run the pattern. By having the client imagine seeing herself in the chair and watching herself on TV, we are causing a double dissociation. This makes it much harder for the client to re-associate into the emotion of the memory.

The movie is old, grainy, and black and white so that the client doesn't associate emotionally with it and so that it symbolizes something old. By running it backward, we are encouraging different neuronal connections, as well as changing the emotional attachment, to the memory she had been replaying for years.

Adding circus music engages a very different set of biochemicals from those associated with the act of visualization, adding to the emotional disconnect. The coach has the client associate into the movie while it's running backward to make it even more difficult for her to relate to it in the old way. The coach makes a joke to add to the resource state (dopamine, attention density . . .) and while the client is in that state, the coach has her run the movie again (step four).

Ultimately, being in control of yourself means being in control of your emotions, which means being able to release any negative emotions that are not serving you in a useful way, and instead feeling how you want to feel, when you want to feel it.

The same is true for your clients. And isn't it interesting to know that, because of mirror neurons, you and your client will likely be feeling the same set of emotions during a session?

Your client may have had many years to cultivate her negative emotions so you better make sure you're in control of your positive, resourceful ones!

Chapter 9: Left-Brain and Right-Brain— Hemispheric Specialization

Are you more left-brained or right-brained? This question makes most neuroscientists cringe. There's been so much misinformation about the two hemispheres of the brain that most of us are left in a state of bilateral confusion. In one study by researchers at the University of Utah, the brains of over 1,000 subjects were studied to determine if one hemisphere was dominant. The researchers found that, while activity was sometimes greater in certain regions, both halves of the brain were essentially equal in their activity. [Rogers M. Researchers debunk myth of "right brain" and "left-brain" personality traits. University of Utah, Office of Public Affairs. Available at http://www.plosone.org/article/info%3Adoi%2F10.1371%2Fj ournal.pone.0071275. Accessed January 22, 2014.]

It's true that both hemispheres process different aspects of information. For example, the left hemisphere processes syntax and other features of language, but the right hemisphere determines the emotional meaning, intonation, and metaphoric significance of the communication. What matters most are the connections between the two.

The hemispheres are separated by a strip of white matter called the corpus callosum. This barrier carries signals as response-potentials from one hemisphere to the other and is crucial in connecting the different aspects of information into a more cohesive whole.

Much of our early knowledge about the two hemispheres of the brain is based on the work of Roger Wolcott Sperry (1913-1994), who received the Nobel Prize for medicine and physiology in 1981 for his work with "split-brain" patients. These were persons who suffered from epilepsy and had surgery to sever the corpus callosum to prevent seizures from moving from one side of the brain to the other. This, in turn, prevented the seizures from happening entirely.

Sperry's early research was on cats. Sperry would sever the corpus callosum and also one of the optic nerves of a cat (cruel, we know) so that the left eye would only transmit information to the left-brain and the right eye to the right-brain. Sperry then ran a series of tests, essentially proving that what had been learned with the right eye could not be passed to the left brain and vice versa. He basically demonstrated that each hemisphere of the brain learned and operated separately when not joined by the corpus callosum.

So, why do we have what amounts to two duplicate brains, one on the left and one on the right? It makes sense that we would have multiple pairs of socks and maybe even two cars, one to take the kids to school and another to be a sporty runaround for evenings out. But why two brains? Nobody really knows but there are at least two possible explanations.

The first explanation is that, as our ancestors moved up the evolutionary ladder, they had to look for food while, at the same time, avoid becoming food. Some research done in chicks, although maybe a little weird, supports this theory. Chicks operating with only one half of their brain were tested to see if they could identify food and predators. They were able to do either task but not both at the same time, whereas their "two-brained" brethren (the control batch of chicks) were able to hunt for food with one half of their brains while the other half kept watch. [Rogers LJ. Light input and the reversal of functional lateralization in the chicken brain. *Behavioural Brain Research*. 1990;38(3):211-21.] Similarly, if you have ever been to Sea World you may have seen the beluga whales and been told that, in order for a whale to sleep and dream, each half of its brain sleeps while the other half keeps watch.

The second explanation for why we have two brains is a little more interesting than the first explanation for change workers: The left-brain and the right-brain each have somewhat more specialized functions. These functions overlap (and the overlap is probably more than authors of "left-brain-right-brain" books would wish to admit), but the functions of the two are not identical. For example, you are processing these words with your left brain . . .

These specializations arise out of structural differences between the two halves. For example, Broca's area and Wernicke's area, the primary areas for processing symbolic language such as human speech, are located in the left brain for most people, but there are other differences as well. For example; the right brain has a greater concentration of axons (brain cell connectors) than the left brain. This means that the left hemisphere has greater processing power, but the right has greater potential connectivity.

Think of this as if each neuron in the left brain is essentially wired to the next one, making very small circuits that are strongly wired together, while the right-brain's wiring is longer, reaching different areas. So, the left-brain is better at the step-by-step, logical type of processing. The right-brain tends to make global insights, connecting diverse bits of information from different parts of the brain.

This means that the left-brain is very good at processing something step-by-step, in depth; it will know everything about a particular thing or subject but that subject won't be linked to another area. The left brain is more linear and detail-oriented, but the right-brain has longer connections so it's more likely to express things like, "The quality of mercy is like a gentle rain." It may not make logical sense to the left brain, but it sounds perfectly reasonable to the right brain.

Switching Between Hemispheres

If you want someone to use the left-brain, ask for details about things. A common example of using the left brain is doing math, but even this example is not accurate because the left-brain does the adding while the right-brain may do the multiplication. This is because the ability to multiply is associated with memory and that memory is often associated with a song memorized by children, and this activity is more of a right-brain function.

If when doing a trance induction, you say something like, "I'd like you to see a staircase, and imagine counting the steps as you walk down . . ."that's a left-brain induction, at least as far as the counting goes. But if you say, "I'd like you to become seven times more relaxed," that's a right-brain induction. What does "seven times more relaxed' even mean? The left-brain says, "I don't even understand the question!" The right-brain says, "I'll deal with that. I know what seven times means and I know what relaxation is. I'll just link those two up."

Asking a person to count is engaging left-brain activity in that person, whereas asking a person to multiply is engaging right-brain activity. Asking a person to focus on something read engages the person's left-brain activity, whereas thinking visually engages the right-brain. One goal toward coaching the entire mind is to lead the client into left-brain activity followed by right-brain activity: left–right–left–right.

If a client says, "First of all, I did this, and, then, this happened, and, then, I did this . . ." and explains the problem logically and sequentially, she is leaning more heavily on the left brain, at least consciously. In this case, it's going to be very hard for such a client to find a solution if she hasn't already, because left-brain processing makes it hard to land somewhere new long enough to link up two new ideas. The art is in being able to switch the client from left-brain to right-brain thinking when needed.

We also have clients who come in and are all over the place. They're processing primarily from the right-brain and make seemingly random connections between unrelated things. Or, if they're stuck in depression, they may be making global statements such as, "nothing will ever be good; these things always happen to me . . ." In these cases, you're going to engage the left brain because it's more action-oriented. This is where more active pattern interrupts, such as tapping or bilateral stimulation, come in handy.

Client's words such as "nothing," "never," and "always," come from the right brain. They are generalizations. When clients use these words, say, "Give me a specific example," which invites the left-brain to get involved by identifying a specific time and place when the problem occurs. Then ask, "Aside from that, how do you want to be that's anything other than how you've been?" This takes clients back into right-brain thinking— because the left can't possibly make sense of this kind of question—but a different part of the right brain is activated. If a client says something like, "I want a sense of confidence." Flip it back to the left-brain by saying, "When was a specific time and place that you felt confident . . ." So, it's always a matter of switching from left, right, left, right.

Through research on stroke and other brain injuries, science has learned a lot about left-brain/right-brain preferences. Strokes usually take place in one side of the brain or the other. For example, the right brain is a little bit more pessimistic than the left brain, which is more optimistic. So, it has been observed that someone who has had a left-brain stroke tends to feel that the stroke was the worst thing that ever happened and that life is over. That person's thinking is an example of global thinking and is being processed by the right brain. In contrast, the person who has had a right-brain stroke feels like the event is not that big a problem. The right brain and left-brain have different takes on optimism.

An overactive right brain is associated with depression, but this does not mean that the right brain is always pessimistic; it's not—it's creative and metaphoric and also has a tendency of being a little more passive. The left-brain is more active. If someone is depressed and that person manages to get out of bed and move around, different areas in the left brain light up, which makes it easier for the person to shift into a more positive state.

When we make these generalizations about brain function, we are really oversimplifying. If researchers were to look at your brain while you were doing something, they would not see only one part of it light up. That's very rare. They would see concentrated activity happening in a certain location, but the brain wave activity is happening throughout the brain. Both halves of your brain are used for all activities [Toga AW, Thompson PM. Mapping brain asymmetry. *Nature Reviews Neuroscience*. 2003;4(1):37-48.] But our generalization about right-brain/left-brain function is a useful metaphor for change work.

Other Differences Between Left-Brain and Right-Brain Function

186

While your left brain tends to use the fovea of your eye to look at detail, your right brain wants to look at everything. The left brain prefers the foreground and right brain, the background. Your left brain processes words and grammar, your right brain listens for tone and modulation of the sound. The right-brain also processes words but has problems with grammar. [Kandel E, et al. eds. *Principles of Neuroscience*. New York: McGraw Hill Medical. 2013.]

Singing is generally a right-brain activity. If someone stutters, that person can still sing. If someone has a stroke or some other kind of damage that affects the language part of the brain, that person can also still sing. Singing is one of those activities that engages both sides of the brain as long as the songs sung include lyrics.

These are all generalizations but useful nonetheless. Remember, a fMRI will just show where activity in the brain is flowing, but it will not provide that much detailed information. If you want to understand left-brain/right-brain specialization from the inside out, read My Stroke of Insight: A Brain Scientist's Personal Journey by Jill Bolte Taylor [New York: Viking Penguin. 2008]. She's a neuroscientist who had a stroke and was able to give an amazing account of what it was like from the inside and from the perspective of a neuroscientist. You can also check out her TED talk on the subject at http://www.ted.com/talks/jill_bolte_taylor_s_powerful_stroke_of_insight.html. It's brilliant.

Having laid the groundwork of left-brain/right-brain specialization, we are now going to talk about our favorite topic, the conscious and unconscious minds. It's not completely accurate to say that the right brain is the unconscious and left brain is the conscious, but it has some truth, and it's a good metaphor. In order to use this metaphor, let's look again at some of the preferences of the left brain and right brain.

The left brain:

- Sees detail
- Focuses on the foreground
- Breaks complicated things down into their component parts
- Is more optimistic
- Is more analytical and logical
- Is better able to deal with time-sensitive projects
- Deals with language

The right-brain:

- Focuses on the big picture
- Focuses on the background
- Makes connections more easily
- Is more pessimistic
- Is more creative
- Is more emotional
- Is better able to find its way around in space
- Deals with abstraction

Those readers familiar with Milton Erickson's work will recognize his conscious–unconscious dissociation pattern in left-brain/right-brain preferences.

Milton Erickson said, "The problem belongs to the conscious mind, the solution belongs to the unconscious mind." Perhaps what he was saying is, "The problem belongs to the left brain. The solution belongs to the right brain." So why is that? Well, it's because the left brain is very good at solving problems. If a problem is the kind that the left brain can solve, it will. It needs access to the right-brain, though, which has all the links to the different parts of the brain and can creatively connect novel solutions—because your right-brain does more than think outside the box. It doesn't even know there is a box.

The reason master NLP trainer John Overdurf asks, "What's everything else that's not that?" is because that sort of question directly engages the right-brain, all those long-ranging links. Remember, we're not trying to create new learnings but link up to what the client already knows. She already knows the problem and already has the resource, but the problem and the resource are not linked on a neurological level. Our job is to help the client make this link.

If you ask, "What's everything else that's not that?" and the client says, "I don't know," you could ask, "What's everything else that's apart from anything you don't know?" The left brain runs away from a question like this, leaving the right brain to spin down those long neural connections to somewhere else, somewhere new, where a resource might lie.

There are several ways in which we can draw on the client's right-brain skills. One way is using conscious-unconscious dissociation. This is a classic Ericksonian hypnosis technique that simply begins by listing the relative strengths of the conscious, left brain and unconscious right brain. Use a slightly different tonality for the conscious and the unconscious. Doing so has the interesting effect of priming and engaging attention from both hemispheres.

Alternatively, you can use location to distinguish left-brain and right-brain phrases by simply moving your head slightly, one way to list the left-brain strengths and the other way to list the right-brain strengths. This was the technique favored by Milton Erickson, who was tone deaf so he couldn't use tonality to distinguish between the two. By marking out both hemispheres with different tonality or location, you are setting up a foundation for the interspersal method of multi-level communication.

Although language processing is primarily in the left hemisphere, the right-brain processes tonality, rhythm, and the emotional and metaphoric aspects of language. So, when we do a trance induction, using shifting tonality and tempo, we can be a lot more cognizant of the different hemispheres we are stimulating.

Here's an example of how to use this with a client:

> "Until now, you've been trying to solve this problem consciously, *but your unconscious has all your resources.*
>
> The conscious mind is quite limited and can only be aware of small bits of information at a time *but your unconscious processes millions of options simultaneously* . . .
>
> Although your conscious mind sees details, it can get lost in them, *but your unconscious gets the big picture and can be more creative in finding solutions.*
>
> Your conscious tends to focus on the problem and what's wrong while *your unconscious can be aware of everything else, so it's easier to focus on what's right.*"

As we have already seen, you can also use inductive language patterns to stimulate the right brain, such as "what is everything else that you haven't been paying attention to . . ." Because of the left-brain's preference for serial processing, it avoids questions with words such as "everything" because it would take the left-brain a ridiculously long time to identify "everything." In contrast, the right-brain is quite happy with this sort of word because its tendency for parallel processing and linking many areas together. The client is, therefore, likely to find an answer to her question or problem in the right

190

brain's abilities.

Ultimately, our goal is to get both sides of the client's brain to work together. Another way to accomplish this is bilateral stimulation, which happens when you get both sides of the body moving to activate both hemispheres. Bilateral stimulation is utilized in many different therapeutic modalities, from eye movement desensitization and reprocessing (EMDR) and EFT to binaural beats and brain synchronization technologies

A simple example of a bilateral stimulation exercise is passing a ball from one hand to the other in such a way that it crosses the center-line of the body. Because chronic anxiety and depression cause an over-activation of the right hemisphere, bilateral stimulation is an excellent pattern interrupt to balance out both halves of the brain. Here's an example from a workshop of how to teach bilateral stimulation as a pattern interrupt:

Demo and Excerpt from a Workshop:

Melissa: Can you take a moment and access a state of anxiety. Whatever anxiety, you don't have to tell us what it is. So, as you're accessing it now, zero to 10, where would you put that?

Client: Probably a four.

Melissa: Can you crank it up to a five? A six?

[The student nods her head.]

Melissa: And now, just follow me. Do this. [Melissa begins passing a ball from the right hand to the left hand and back, moving the left hand out to the left as the left hand takes the ball, and then the right hand out to the right as the right hand takes the ball, and the student mirrors her.] That's right. We're just passing it back and forth. The reason this works is because anxiety tends to be primarily on one hemisphere of the brain.

191

When we do this, we're accessing right-brain . . . left-brain . . . right-brain . . . left-brain. Now, there's so much activity happening in the brain that that anxiety you had can't keep itself together. So, this one feels like a reset button for me. Almost like a neutral position. It's just a way of stopping that. Stop. Notice how you feel.

Client: I still feel some.

Melissa: Where is it now?

Client: Three or four.

Melissa: Can you crank it up a little more?

Client: Yeah.

Melissa: Now, what I want you to do is to relax your shoulders just a little bit as you do this. [Both Melissa and the student resume passing balls back and forth.] As long as you're crossing the middle of your body, you're good. Doesn't have to be a ball. Can be a pen, water bottle, the keys in your pocket. Anything will work as long as you cross the middle of your body, you're stimulating both hemispheres. Take a moment and notice when it shifts. Got it? Now stop and check in. Where is it now?

Client: Probably a two.

Melissa: A two? So we go again. And what we're doing is just conditioning the change in. I could ask her to crank it up again, but I want to move on, and she's smiling and looks far more relaxed so I know it's cool to leave it. [To student] We're good? Check in?

Client: Good.

Melissa: [Turning to class] So, there's a few different things I'm doing while teaching this. I'm relaxing my own body, sending a signal to her unconscious to do the same. And I'm starting to use language to stack the deck. "The reason why this is working . . ." as I subtly shift my tone of voice and nod my head, making this more of an embedded command. And then, I dip into a little bit more sing-song tonality, almost a lullaby as I say, "right-brain . . . left-brain . . . right-brain . . . left-brain," which engages a different area of the right brain. When I say, "that anxiety you had," I'm using spatial and temporal language; "that" creates distance and "had" shifts it subtly into the past. Most importantly, I am getting to a state where I feel relaxed. I'm assuming her mirror neurons are firing off as well. It becomes a way of engaging the brain. By explaining bilateral stimulation, it makes it easier for people to accept such a simple and silly technique. "Stimulating both hemispheres to shift neural activity," sounds a hell of a lot better than, "Passing a ball back and forth."

This exercise is also a pattern interrupt. We can use it for anything. This is step three of Dr. Schwartz's Four-Step Protocol. It dissociates the client from the problem feeling as she does something other than her normal habit. This technique is immediately accessible and far more efficient than you would think. Melissa has had clients stop full-blown panic attacks by using this technique.

By passing the ball, we are having the client take action, which is associated more with the left hemisphere [Wunderlich K., et al. Neural computations underlying action-based decision making in the human brain. *Proceedings of the National Academy of Science of the USA*, 106: 17,199-17,204] When you can get people who are depressed to do something, just to move, you're starting to activate and balance out the brain. It's pretty interesting that most of these things require some action. Even Dr. Schwartz protocol is "do a different activity." Whether it's gardening, or exercising, it usually requires moving because the

193

right hemisphere is associated with withdrawal whereas the left moves forward. This may be a little simplistic, but if you think of it this way, it allows you to be more creative.

Melissa always explains this to her clients when they are talking about activating both sides of the brain. The best and easiest way to change a state is to change the physiology. In order to do this technique, you have to sit up straight and engage peripheral vision. When you teach it, you want to model the physiology for the client: relax and visibly relax your jaw, which helps activate the parasympathetic nervous system as well. When you drop your jaw a little bit more, it stimulates the vagus nerve, which goes through the feedback system that tells your heart, your lungs, and your gastrointestinal system to relax. Steven Porges's book Polyvagal Theory: Neurophysiological Foundations of Emotions, Attachment, Communication, and Self-Regulation [New York: W. W. Norton & Company, Inc.; 2011] is a fascinating read that covers this in depth.

Separate Minds: The WADA Test

The blood flow to each part of the brain is separate so surgeons can put one half of the brain to sleep and keep the other half awake. Doing so is called the Wada test. The left-brain generally does the talking, but if surgeons put your left-brain to sleep, your right-brain can talk, or rather it gets the opportunity to talk. Using the Wada test, as well as questioning stroke patients who have had the left and right hemispheres of their brains surgically separated, researchers can discover a lot about the preferences of each half of the brain.

Shawn heard a great story about a patient undergoing the Wada test whose right brain could talk. (He hasn't been able to track down the story so it could be apocryphal.) There was an accountant who loved his job, but when the surgeon put his left-brain to sleep and asked him, "What do you want to do?" he said, "I want to be a stock car driver." So, his right-brain had a lifelong dream of being a stock car racer, and his left-brain was an accountant. We love this story: the accountant and the stock car racer sharing the same body!

Hemispheric Disagreement

There are a number of neuroscientists who argue that hemispheric disagreement can be the cause of several psychological problems, Dr. Jack Pettigrew, from the University of Queensland, argues that manic-depression is caused by switching from manic left brain to depressed right brain.

Even with a non-split brain, we find the left brain and right brain disagreeing about the direction a person should take: one hemisphere may opt for safety while the other may opt for adventure; one hemisphere may wish to live for the moment, but the other may want to plan ahead. These types of hemispheric disagreements may manifest themselves in a sort of problem in which the client says, "On the one hand I want to do this, but on the other hand I want to do that instead."

When there is hemispheric disagreement, how do we go about reaching a resolution? If we simply invite the client to debate the pros and cons of each approach, we are most likely allowing her to favor the left-brain thinking, which has the most control over speech and logical thinking. If we simply allow the client to go with an emotional gut feeling or envision the possibilities of life, we may be allowing her to favor right brain thinking, which tends to deal with emotion and visualization.

An approach that balances the cognitive left brain with the creative right brain is needed. Now, we don't know if the concept of hemispheric disagreement is literally true, but it's certainly a great metaphor. We have a pattern in NLP called the Visual Squash that balances conscious and unconscious processing, left-brain and right-brain activities.

The Visual Squash

The visual squash essentially takes an either/or dilemma that the client faces and splits it into the two choices. So, the client might say, "On the one hand I would like to take some time off and travel, but on the other hand, I don't want to leave my job . . ."

In this case, we would take one of the choices, "traveling," and represent it as an image held on either the left or the right hand, and the other choice, "stay in my current job," represented as an image on the other hand. We then find the highest positive intention of each of these choices, which will typically overlap to a significant degree. We can then share resources between the two sides and reintegrate them into the client. If all goes to plan, then the client will be able to act from the shared highest positive intention, which is a new value incorporating the benefits of both choices. (You can read more about the Visual Squash in Shawn's book, NLP Mastery: The Visual Squash [New York: Changing Minds Publishing. 2014.].

Understanding that this sort of client dilemma may be caused by hemispheric disagreement allows us to perform the Visual Squash pattern with a lot more precision than we might otherwise do. Many practitioners do a Visual Squash as a cognitive left-brain pattern. But if the theory is correct that the split between "on the one hand and on the other hand" is a left-brain/right-brain split, then we don't want to do this in an entirely cognitive way because, if we do, we haven't really resolved it. All we've done is taken sides. We've reinforced one half of the client's brain at the expense of the other.

Instead, we make sure that we do something visual, then something language-based, then something specific, then something peripheral, then some listing of attributes, then some "everything else." So, we can now think of the issue as being a disagreement between verbal and visual, between literal and symbolic, between logical and emotional, between words and tonality, between deductive and inductive, and so on, representing all the specializations of the left brain and right brain, respectively.

Performing the Visual Squash

To perform visual squash in this new way, we will first seek to find which part of the dilemma is more associated with the left brain and which with the right brain. For example, if the client wants, in part, to stay at her current job and, in part, wants to leave, we can ask: "What is the name of the part that wants to stay? What is the name of the part that wants to leave?"

This is left-brain activity because we are labeling the parts, and naming is a left-brain activity.

At the same time, we can be listening to the tonality that the client uses when describing the parts. Remember tonality is a right-brain activity. We can ask, "What's the image of the part that wants you to stay?"

This usually engages right-brain activity because it requires visualization, unless the client says, "I see myself working at my current job," in which case, the more literal left brain may have answered.

"What is the benefit, the positive intention, of that part?" [Left brain]

"How do you feel about that part?" [Right brain]

"What is specific to that part?" [Left brain]

"What is everything else that's not that part?" [Right brain]

"What do you think is going on with that?" [Left brain]

"What do you feel is going on?" [Right-brain]

When a coach has a great deal of left and right-brain information, she can begin to encourage the dialogue between the two hemispheres utilizing the symbolic as well as the linguistic elements of each:

"What do you feel about that thought? What do you think about that feeling? What's everything else that's not that thought? Please be more specific about that feeling."

Here's a demo of this pattern with a client who wants to stop drinking alcohol:

Client: Part of me really wants to quit drinking, but the other part is afraid to try.

Coach: Can you put your hands out in front of you, palms up? Good. Now, in the left hand imagine the part of you that wants to stop drinking and in the right, the part of you that is afraid to try. Can you imagine that?

[Client nods yes]

Coach: Good. Now, create an image for both parts in each hand. What are the names of those two parts?

Client: The part that wants to quit is named Christine, and the part that's afraid to is Chrissy.

Coach: And how does Christine feel to you?

Client: Strong, confident.

Coach: And what's the positive intention of Christine wanting to stop drinking?

Client: Um, to be healthier and more clear and productive.

Coach: And when you are healthier, clear, and productive, how do you feel?

Client: Good. Powerful.

Coach: And when you feel good and powerful, where do you feel that in your body?

Client: In my chest and shoulders, I feel an expansion in my whole body.

Coach: And when you feel this expansion and you are clear and productive, what does that do for you?

Client: It keeps me moving forward towards my goals.

Coach: As you move forward towards your goals, what's everything else that you hadn't been feeling that you can now?

[The client visibly relaxes and dips into an altered state]

Coach: That's right. And as you notice all that, what do you think this part really wants for you?

Client: To be happy and strong.

Coach: That's right. And on the other hand, what is the positive intention of the part you named Chrissy?

Client: Um . . . to help me be more sociable and connected to other people. Drinking helps me to feel more relaxed in social situations.

Coach: And when you are more relaxed, sociable, and connected to other people, how do you feel?

Client: Comfortable. My body feels relaxed in my shoulders especially.

Coach: And when you are feeling more relaxed and comfortable, socially connecting, what does that do for you?

Client: It helps me to fit in with my colleagues.

Coach: And when you are fitting in, relaxed, and comfortable, what's everything else you can feel that you haven't been seeing? And when you know that, what does that do for you?

Client: It makes me feel happy.

Coach: Now, turning your palms to face each other, allow your conscious and your unconscious to integrate all the positive intentions of both parts so that you create something so much stronger, happier, and productive than those parts alone.

[The client's hands start slowly moving together as she relaxes into a deeper trance state.

Coach: That's right. As your conscious and unconscious begin to come together, you can feel more relaxed as you move toward your goals, allowing yourself to be connecting to everyone in a more clear and powerful way . . . taking time to notice how you feel as you see yourself stronger . . . noticing what you think about these things coming together as specific steps might come to mind as you feel those hands getting closer together . . .

[The clients hands come together]

Coach: And bring this integration up to your heart, and feel how good it feels. What do you think about that?

Client: Wow. That was really strange. My hands seemed to be moving on their own. I wasn't doing it! And what was really cool is, I saw both parts coming together so the younger, scared part merged and grew up into the powerful confident part. Amazing how that all happened.

Coach: And when you think about stopping drinking now, how do you feel?

Client: I feel kind of excited. It's like, I don't need to rely on that to help me feel strong and relaxed. I'm feeling like I will connect better with everyone if I'm clear-headed.

Research shows that the left-right brain split has been over-sold by the popular science publishing industry. And yet your left logical brain tells you that the left-right divide holds some truth, and your right metaphorical brain tells you that it provides a powerful set of metaphors and experiences for creating change. So embrace it with both sides of your brain and discover, how it can inform your change-work!

Chapter 10: Learning: Movement and Space within Human Experience

In this chapter we are going to talk about how space and movement through it is part of our unconscious human experience. As you'll see, understanding how space is processed in the brain will give us clues as to how we construct our problems and how we can build solutions in the same way.

A baby is born. Let's call her Mia. Mia has limited ability to move in space because she has not yet learned how to walk or even crawl. Yet she, like most babies, is very curious, and begins to move her eyes to explore her environment. Her mother's smiling face comes into view above her. It's blurred at first but then moves closer, and Mia is able to focus on it. Her brain is hard-wired to recognize faces, particularly smiling faces, and she responds by smiling as well. This moving face is her first experience of the concept of space, to be repeated many times in the bright light of day and the dark of the night.

Later on, Mia will begin to track objects as they move through her visual field from left to right, right to left, near to far, and far to near. As her coordination improves, she will begin reaching out with her hands, perhaps to grasp her mother's finger. And she will learn, in a very tangible and embodied way, that some things are "within reach" and others "out of reach" way before she understands the meaning of those words themselves.

At some point, Mia learns to sit up, aligning her spine to balance the effects of gravity that weighs her down. As she plays, she learns that she can reach out with a spoon to pick up her food or reach out with certain toys to touch things that would otherwise be out of reach. She is beginning to explore the use of tools to make "far" become "near."

One day, Mia finds herself crawling along the floor toward a favorite toy. Her concept of space has changed because she is now able to move to objects that are otherwise out of reach. Her body's ability to move through space has changed everything.

Soon, she will "stand on her own two feet," "take that first step," and "move ahead," although she will have to "learn how to walk before she can run." She is well on her way to "putting her best foot forward." Metaphors of space and movement are useful tools that we use in our everyday speech without considering where they come from.

Perhaps a client comes to see us because she is "feeling down," "carrying the weight of the world on her shoulders." Perhaps she looks back on dark memories or feels the future is closed to her. With our help, she leaves the office" feeling uplifted," "on top of the world," looking forward to a bright and "open" future.

Coaching Trick

Because our clients use space to construct their problems, it is good to know that there are many ways to use spatial language to move their attention around. The first thing to do is to listen to how they are constructing the problem by paying attention to the clues they offer you in the language they choose. For example, one client may feel "overwhelmed," another may be "holding onto" an issue, and a third may "face a barrier" to further progress.

If a client says she is feeling overwhelmed, then by taking the words literally, you know that the client represents her problem as being on top or over her. The next question should be something that allows the client to get "out from under it," even to "get on top of it." Questions would take the form of: "Over and above that, what haven't you been considering?"

Other clients may carry their problems around with them wherever they go, even making the problem part of their identity, "I have anxiety," or "I am a failure." We can help them to lay their problems down, at least for a little while, by asking questions such as, "Aside from that, what are some of the outcomes you want to have?" or "What's everything else you are that's anything but that?" . . . "How will you be when you can let go of all that?"

If they face a barrier, making statements such as "It's like I'm banging my head against a brick wall," then you may want to take them, "Over and beyond that . . . or "aside from that . . ." Or, you can ask them, "What do you imagine is on the other side of that?"

Because the unconscious mind uses space and movement as metaphor, even simple language patterns, based on a literal spatial interpretation of what they said, can have wonderful positive effects. Remembering this when working with clients lets you manipulate the internal landscape of the clients' problems in a way that is accessible to the unconscious mind.

Research on Spatial Metaphors

Metaphors of space are well known and have been extensively researched by linguists such as George Lakoff and Mark Johnson (Metaphors We Live By. Chicago: University of Chicago Press. 1980), and Steven Pinker (The Stuff of Thought: Language as a Window to Human Nature. New York: Penguin Group. 2007). We think according to space, presumably because we originally had to learn where to go to find food and where not to go to avoid becoming food. Movement and space play particular evolutionary roles in learning.

There are a number of spatial metaphors that are common across many contexts, cultures and languages. For example, "up" generally has positive implications: "rise above," "pick yourself up," and "higher ground." In contrast, "down" generally has negative implications: "he looks down on me," "I feel down," "I'm depressed," "he came down on me like a ton of bricks," and "I wouldn't stoop to her level." After all, they say, heaven is above us and hell is below.

Right is generally positive, right? An adroit metaphor there. Left is more negative, gauche ("left" in French), even sinister ("left" in Latin). Politics not included . . .

Forward generally represents the future. Moving forward is often considered to be positive: "I'm moving ahead," "Let's move forward," and "I'm looking forward to that." Of course, a person could also "be moving forward toward disaster" and "not be looking forward to that at all."

Backward represents the past: "looking back" "without a backward glance." Moving backward is often negative: "that's a step back," and "back to the dark ages." Of course, a person can "get back to what's important" or wish to be "back in the good old days."

As the above examples show, we can also use space as a metaphor for time. Think of the movie Back to the Future. We will be talking more about time as space (or space as time) later on, or farther ahead, in the chapter, if you prefer.

There is uncertainty about the degree to which spatial metaphors are "hard-wired" into our brains at birth and how much is developed by our experience in the world as we grow up, but neuroscientific research is beginning to shed light on how our brains are organized for space and how space and learning are related. For example, memorizing a path through space—through a landscape, that is—appears to be laid down in memory via a pathway that is different to other types of memory. Fascinating research has been done on London cab drivers regarding this, as we mentioned in the earlier chapter on memory. We will now examine this research a little more closely.

Looking back on how London developed as a city from pre-Roman times to the present, it is easy to understand how the streets developed following ancient pathways, curving around hallowed landmarks, to become a virtual maze the logic of which defied common sense or memorization in pre-GPS days. Yet London cabbies have to not only know where every place is, but also the shortest route between any two points, from A to Z as it were.

In order to become a London cabbie, you have to have the "Knowledge" with a capital K, to be able to describe a route between any two points that is within a whisker of the shortest route. In order to gain the Knowledge, aspiring cabbies spend years traveling round London on a moped. The average cabbie-in-training takes between two and four years memorizing well over 300 core routes: around 25,000 streets and 20,000 landmarks and other points of interest, including palaces, museums, hotels, parks, theaters, and so on.

Scans of the brains of taxi drivers who have completed the Knowledge show a marked increase in size in the right hippocampus where researchers believe a virtual map of the London cityscape is kept. Learning to follow routes through a landscape appears to be a task in which long-term memories are laid down specifically in the hippocampus. Of course, images or pictures of landmarks on the routes might be stored in the visual cortex, but the overall organization of landscape appears to be stored in the hippocampus. This is a very different type of learning.

Because learning a landscape creates a very specific memory, one that is not typically linked to the client's problem, working within a "landscape" can provide a very special type of solution that engages different areas of the brain and therefore brings new mental resources to bear. The solutions are maintained in areas of the brain that are much older than the neocortex or the PFC and separate from the more emotive centers. Creating a route through a landscape that leads from the problem to the solution provides a unique and fascinating way to create change.

Landscapes can be created and explored with a client using modalities such as Blending Space, Clean Language, or simply using guided visualizations. We will talk more about each of these later.

Near and Far

Other research shows a link between the structure of the brain and the concepts of "near" and "far." Research shows that the brain considers something to be near if we can reach it; for example if the object is within arm's reach [Colby CL and

Duhamel JR. Spatial representations for action in parietal cortex. *Cognitive Brain Research.* 1996;5(1-2):105-15.] Not only does the brain distinguish where an object is relative to the hand or limb, but also where an object is relative to the visual field (so we know where to look), the head (in case it is dangerous perhaps), and the mouth (in case it is good to eat)! In contrast, the object will be coded differently within the brain if it is farther away, out of reach. Response will be less immediate. We can use this difference in coding using submodalities from NLP.

To get a grasp on this, consider something that you might wish to eat, such as a cupcake. When you think about it, you may imagine it in your hand, right in front of you, close to your mouth. Yum! However if you imagine it being behind you, it's not so attractive. If you are imagining it being behind you, on the ground, on the other side of the room, it's really unattractive!

Using Near and Far with NLP Submodalities

As we now know, the brain codes things differently depending on whether they are near, within arm's length, or far, out of arm's length. The location of an imagined image in our mind is called a submodality of the picture in NLP. Remember, a submodality is simply a quality of the picture. A picture that you make inside your mind appears to have a certain location in the outside world, perhaps it is a little to the left or more to the right. It could be a little higher or a little farther down. It may be nearer, or farther away. The picture can also be framed or unframed, in two dimensions like a photograph or three dimensions, still or like a movie, color or black and white, big or small. These are all visual submodalities.

If you want to experience this now, think about someone who you really like, perhaps someone who you love. See a picture of the person in your mind. Notice where the picture is: to the right, center, or to the left, higher or lower, closer or farther away. Notice other qualities of the picture such as whether it is in color or black-and-white. Is it framed or unframed? Is it a movie or still?

Now think about someone who you don't like, and see a picture of that person. Where is that picture? You'll probably find it in a different location to the picture you just visualized of the person you love. Notice the other qualities of the second picture and compare them to the first. Some qualities may be the same and some different. Now blank the screen and think about the first person you visualizes, the one you really like!

Asking about the location of a picture is one of the most significant and useful things we can ask a client: "When you think about that, where is the picture?" The client will often show you with her eyes, which will literally look in the direction of the picture and focus on the point in space where it is.

Remember, when we say location, we don't mean "inside the head" (although it obviously is), we mean where does the picture appear to be in the space around the client. We talk more about using location within the visual sense in Chapter 6, which discusses the visual cortex, but please be aware that simply knowing and being able to change the location and other submodalities of internal pictures and sounds can produce amazing results all by themselves.

The next time a client is talking about a problem, ask her where the picture is. Chances are that that the client will indicate the space in front of her. Go further and ask the client how close the picture she sees is, and you will usually find that it's within arm's length (because if it wasn't, it probably wouldn't be a problem for her!). An alternative mode is one in which the client finds herself associated into the picture so that it is panoramic whereby objects within the scene will be as close or distant as they are in reality. If the picture she is visualizing is more like photograph, though, it will probably be within arm's length.

A simple but highly effective piece of change work involves simply asking the client to move the picture away. If you ever watched or listened to a demonstration by Richard Bandler, the brilliant c-founder of NLP, you will notice that his very first gambit is often to ask about the location of the image of the problem and then to ask the client to move it farther away.

Think again of the image of the person you love. Notice what happens when you move the image farther away. Now bring it back in close and feel the difference. Take the image of the person you don't like, and you will likely feel relief when you push it way out into the distance.

The farther away the picture moves, the less emotional impact it is likely to have, but moving the picture just out of arm's reach also can be effective because the brain recodes it as "out of reach." Here's a demonstration:

Coach: As you think of the problem, where is the picture?

Client: It's here [gesturing in front]

Coach: Is it framed or unframed?

Client: It's all around me . . .

Coach: Okay, and if you were to see it like a photograph or a picture, how big would it be?

Client: About this . . .[indicates a rectangle about 18 inches high]

Coach: And how close?

Client: Close [indicates a place well within arm's length]

Coach: Okay, now I want you to move the picture away until it is there [indicating a location just outside the client's arm's length]

Client: Okay . . .

Coach: How is it now?

Client: Hmmm, it doesn't seem such a big deal now . . .

Coach: Okay, now move it even farther away, move it so that it's way over there. What happens then?

Client: I can't seem to connect to it emotionally. It doesn't seem important at all . . .

Optimal Goal Setting

Imagine something that is already within reach. Perhaps you have ordered something from Amazon.com and it is in the mail to you. Do you feel the same level of excitement that you felt when you were deciding whether or not to buy it? Have you ever seen something in the store that you simply had to have, but when you got it home it stayed in the bag for a week?

Imagine a goal you have that will take years to achieve, perhaps a college degree that is four years of effort away or even next year's vacation. How far away is that picture? You may notice that the picture appears very distant (or perhaps blurred), and you may find it difficult to get excited and motivated by these too-distant goals. The degree is broken down into more manageable chunks, such as "next semester" or the vacation is forgotten until it's a week away and its remembrance suddenly swims into view.

If goals are already within reach, we are not motivated to take action because we practically have them already, but if they are too far away, they may feel too distant to motivate us. This is another aspect of our brains coding "near" and "far." In the case of too near, we feel we already have it; in the case of too far, we are not motivated to take action to access it.

But there is a middle ground, out of reach, but close enough to grasp if we move, if we take action. Look around and put your attention on something within reach, and you may feel your hand want to move toward it as if to pick it up. Now look round and put your attention on something that is just out of reach. You may find your body begins to lean toward it!

This idea can be used for goal setting. Ask the client to imagine a goal and ask her where the picture is and how motivated she feels to "go for it." Try moving the goal closer so it is easily within reach. How does that change the client's motivation? Now move the goal much farther away so that it seems distant. How motivated is the client? Finally move the goal so that it is just a little out of the client's reach, a few inches beyond arm's length. Now how motivated is the client?

You can also try moving the goal so that it is a little down, as in "downhill" in the visualized picture. For many people, this changes the motivation towards the goal by creating the sensation of the momentum of the pull of walking downhill. Sometimes moving an image of a negative trigger, such as a beer or piece of cake, uphill also changes a person's motivation about that trigger. However, also note that, for others, placing a goal uphill in a visualized picture makes it more attractive because the goal may be seen as a challenge. Make exploring your client's strategies a fun part of your sessions. By making the client as curious as you are, half the work is done.

Gestures and Language

The mother puts her fingers to her lips, telling her child to be quiet, the athlete pumps her fist in the air as she crosses the finish line, the film director places his hand over his heart as he makes his acceptance speech thanking his cast and crew, one customer waves the waiter away with the palm of his hand, another waves the same waiter over.

Gestures represent a very special, and spatial, role in our communications. We move our hands up and down, right and left, show or hide our palms, and touch our belly, chest, throat, mouth, nose, ears, rub our hands together, make a fist. The list of gestures we make is almost endless.

Recent research using fMRIs indicates that gestures and language are both processed in the same regions of the brain, perhaps indicating that spoken language was built on the brain's earlier ability to interpret gesture.

Researchers at the National Institute on Deafness and Other Communication Disorders put volunteers inside a fMRI and showed them movie clips of people either speaking coherently or speaking nonsense. Then they showed the volunteers movies of people using common gestures or making random hand movements. The same brain areas within the inferior frontal and posterior temporal regions were activated by spoken gibberish and random gestures and, also, the same brain areas in the inferior frontal and posterior temporal regions were activated by coherent spoken language and commonly used gestures; however those areas that were activated by gibberish and random gestures differed from those areas activated by coherent language and commonly used gestures. That is, gibberish is processed in the same areas of the brain whether it is spoken gibberish or gestural gibberish, and spoken language and gestures that make sense are also related and process in their own same unique areas of the brain. [Xu J, et al. Symbolic

213

gestures and spoken language are processed by a common neural system. *Proceedings of the National Academy of Sciences.* 2009;106(49):20664-9.]

The theory goes that the posterior temporal area generates a set of possible meanings for the word or gesture, and the inferior frontal gyrus then selects the one that is most appropriate.

Interesting research done at Cornell University by Andrew Bass, a professor of neurobiology, and presented at the annual meeting of the Society for Experimental Biology in 2013 suggests that our spoken language essentially hijacked parts of our brain that were used for gesturing. Even more mind-bending is the fact that Bass's research suggests that these portions of the brain originated in fish, which would move their fins to communicate with fellow fish. As Dory said in the movie Nemo, "When life gets you down, you know what you gotta do? Just keep swimming. Just keep swimming . . ."

This knowledge (the fact that gestures carry meaning, not the film trivia), allows us to use gestures to create meaning while bypassing the conscious mind, which as we know, focuses on words. It also provides a mechanism for the theory of priming, which we discuss separately in Chapter 4, which discussed implicit memory and priming.

Coaching Application

Because gestures carry meaning just as words do, and because the meaning is both communicated and received unconsciously for the most part, we can use gestures to consciously influence the client's unconscious mind.

A great example of this is when we use gestural anchors to trigger a resource state in the client. When you recognize that the client has gotten into a positive emotional state, pay attention to the gestures she uses. On a certain level, each gesture that a client uses represents a particular state of mind. Later in the session, when you make one of the client's particular gestures, it will take the client right back into the mind state that that gesture represents to her. The process by which this takes place utilizes mirror neurons, which we covered in an earlier chapter.

Calibrating to Gestures

Many clients also show you, through their gestures and language, how they have set up their problem. If you listen, you will be able to guide them through their internal metaphors and give them the space to find their own solutions. For instance:

Client: Every time I try to move forward, something stops me [gestures with hands in front].

Coach: And what's it like, this thing that stops you?

Client: A huge brick wall. I keep running up against it . . .

Coach: And aside from that, what do you notice? If you step to the side of the brick wall, what do you imagine?

Client: It seems to extend to the sides . . .

Coach: And if you step back from it, what do you notice?

Client: I have more space . . .

Coach: And above all that, what do you notice?

Client: More room, more space; it feels better.

Coach: And looking down from all that space to where that brick wall was, what are you noticing now?

Client: It seems smaller, for sure, but also not as daunting . . . I can even see room around it, like maybe I could just find a simple way around that.

Coach: And as you imagine moving around that, now, feeling more space, what's the next smallest step you can take towards moving forward with your goal?

Client: Well, it feels like I can just take one step at a time. Write up the outline, then send it to my manager . . .

Coach: And how does that feel?

Client: Good! Easier. That brick wall doesn't even seem to be there . . . How did you do that?

Coach: I didn't do anything. You just expanded your view, and that lends itself to more options . . .

Space as a Context

Living in Manhattan, the authors of this book have the good fortune to be near some of the world's greatest art and museums, such as the Metropolitan Museum of Art. Occasionally, Shawn will take his clients there to talk through an issue in the presence of master painters or sculptors such as Van Gogh, Matisse, Rodin, and many others. Simply being in a wonderful space, surrounded by works of art, brings a new perspective on old issues.

Space, location, and where we are, makes a difference to how we feel about things. You probably remember going on vacation to somewhere beautiful, and as soon as you arrived, all your old problems seemed remote and not so serious after all.

A study was performed by Colin Ellard, professor of experimental psychology at the University of Waterloo in

Canada to test the subjective mental and physiological effects of different environments. Subjects were asked to walk around various locations in New York City, Berlin, and Mumbai. They recorded their subjective emotional experiences as they went and were also wired up with skin conductors to measure more objective data on the level of emotional arousal.

Many of the results were what might be expected, for example, feeling calmer in a garden than in a busy street but the type of garden also impacted the experience. For example, a garden of an older person produced less emotional arousal than a cemetery garden, and this response was perhaps related to the symbolic meanings of cemeteries. Past experiences also seemed to play a part in the responses, with natives of the city being more comfortable with hustle and bustle than visitors. So space itself creates or evokes emotional states.

In fact, being in any space that is different from the one in which the problem normally occurs creates a literal reframe of the problem. Each time the issue is viewed from a different perspective, it can be seen differently. This is why taking a client to a museum can offer a fresh perspective on a problem.

For those familiar with the work of Milton Erickson, you will know that he often "tasked" his clients to climb Squaw Peak, a small mountain that springs up out of the otherwise flat deserts around Phoenix, Arizona, where Milton Erickson practiced in his later life.

For anyone who has climbed Squaw Peak, the views from the top are amazing. Because Phoenix is so hot, the only sensible time to climb the mountain is early, before the sun rises so that you get to experience the dawn when you reach the top. From the parking lot at the bottom of the mountain, you look up at the peak, which doesn't seem particularly high, and may say to yourself, "Is that it? That looks easy!" but as you begin to climb, each time you reach the top of a ridge, you see another

217

ridge in front of you. As you climb farther, with your legs beginning to tire, you wonder whether you'll ever reach the top. Finally, you're there, and when you see the whole of the desert, expansive and breathtaking, you know the opportunity to see the sunrise from that vantage point was well worth the climb.

So, a client's simple act of climbing Squaw Peak, in the context of thinking about her problem, created a powerful reframe.

Blending Space

A blended space is a combination of two different spaces. If you simply went climbing Squaw Peak while reading this book in your living room, you created a blended space of the two.

Once we understand that any two spaces can be blended, powerful possibilities of change work become apparent. Not only can we go to real spaces, we can blend imaginary space with real, symbolic, or metaphoric space.

Exercise (developed by John Overdurf)

Think of an issue you would like to have more insight about. Try this simple exercise: Draw a curve on a piece of paper, something like a bell curve that begins near the left-bottom corner of the paper, moves up toward the top-center as the intensity increase, then down, ending near the right-bottom corner of the paper. Now imagine that this curve represents a small issue or problem that you may have.

As you look at the curve within the context of your problem, notice where your attention is. Do you feel buried underneath the wave or are you being carried towards the peak? Perhaps the wave blocks your way, or else, maybe it's carrying you forward toward the unknown?

Now imagine that you're looking down at the curve from the

top and notice any insights that you have about your issue. The idea is not to try to consciously think of being "above" the problem, but just to be with the space and notice any insights that arise.

Now imagine looking back at the curve from the front. How is that experience different? What about looking forward at the curve from behind? What about if you look down from the front at a 45% angle? . . . Or if you observe the curve from "inside"? How about being in front of the curve, this time looking forward (away from it)? Choose a few more perspectives, and notice how each feels different and brings different insights into the issue.

This fun and interesting exercise demonstrates how our mind uses space in considering issues.

Using Space to Anchor Resources

The idea of space as a context in which our experiences take place gives us wonderful opportunities to blend the space in which the problem or issue normally takes place with another real physical space containing more or different resources. In fact, resources can be assigned to any space we choose using the concept of spatial anchors.

A spatial anchor is an NLP term meaning a specific place or location that becomes associated with a specific state. Spatial anchors are examples of a well-known and widely studied psychological phenomenon called "context-dependent memory." Context-dependent memory means that something learned in a specific context can be better remembered in that context than somewhere new. Think about the last time you could not find your keys. You probably walked around your house or apartment (if that was where you believed you left them), thinking "where did I put my key . . . ?" until you stepped into the living room and suddenly remembered that you had put them on top of the television set. It is being in the context (the living room) that sparks the memory.

The neuroscience of context-dependent learning is not completely understood, although, as with spatial memory, the hippocampus appears to play an important role. The studies that have been performed to track the brain mechanisms responsible suggest that the PFC (remember, that's the "prefrontal cortex) and hippocampus are both involved in the process [Kalisch R, et al. Context-dependent human extinction memory is mediated by a ventromedial prefrontal and hippocampal network. *The Journal of Neuroscience.* 2006;26(37):9503-11.]

Presumably the PFC is asking "Where did I leave my keys . . ." while the hippocampus is waiting for the right contextual triggers before it provides the answer!

A simple way to use spatial anchors with a client is to use two or three different places, perhaps chairs, each representing a different state. For example one place might represent the "problem place," another the "resource place," and a third a "dissociated place." Ask the client to step onto the "problem" place and associate her into the problem, then ask her to step away and onto the dissociated place, and from this more neutral position, ask the client about the resource she would need to solve the problem.

Perhaps the client says that she wants confidence so you begin to associate her into a confident state and ask her to step to the "resource place." When fully associated into a state of confidence, the client then looks back at the "problem place." You can repeat the pattern so that the client steps from one place to another until confidence spreads to all three contexts, and the negative feeling can no longer be accessed.

A similar pattern is the NLP "Disney Strategy" pattern,

developed by Robert Dilts. This is based on a technique actually employed by Walt Disney, who had three rooms in which he worked, one for playful dreaming creativity, one to criticize his own creative ideas, and a third to find solutions to deal with the criticisms and find practical ways to make his dreams come to life.

This strategy can be recreated, albeit on a smaller scale, by having three places in the room, one for each of the "Dreamer," "Critic," and "Realist." In the first Dreamer place, only think creative thoughts and especially do not allow criticism of these ideas or plan how to implement them. In the second, the Critic location, consider only the things that could prevent the Dreamer's ideas from working, and in the third Realist location, consider practical aspects of implementing the Dreamer's ideas and dealing with the Critic's difficulties.

You can cycle through the three positions. For example, ask the Dreamer to find creative ways to solve the Critic's issues as many times as is necessary. In fact, the more you cycle through the three positions, the more context-dependent learning will associate creativity to the Dreamer location, critical thinking to the Critic location, and practicality to the Realist location.

Space-Time

Given that the brain uses space as a metaphor to code experience, it should not be surprising that it also uses space as a metaphor for time. Not only is this principle demonstrated in our language: "moving the event forward by an hour," or "pushing it back to next week," but it is also deeply rooted within our brain structure in ways that are measurable [Gentner D. and Imai M. Is the future always ahead? Evidence for system-mappings in understanding space-time metaphors. Proceedings of 14th Annual Conference of the Cognitive Science Society, July 29-August 1, 1992. pp. 510-515.]

If you would like to experience this for yourself without thinking about it, simply point to your past. Now, point to your future. For most people, the past is either to the left or behind them while the future is either to the right or in front of them.

Cultural differences may be at play with this exercise. For example, many native Hebrew speakers keep the past on their right and the future on their left, presumably because the written language moves from right to left. Similarly, some Asian people keep the past and the future aligned vertically, again presumably because of the way they write.

One way of combining physical movement with a mental landscape is to have the client imagine a timeline on the floor. Have the client choose a spot to stand on that represents the present. Then, ask the client to point to the future and the past. This creates a timeline in which the client is standing in the position of the present moment. We can now have the client literally "walk the line" to do the change work, visiting the past or the future as appropriate.

Remember that movement and action also engage the left hemisphere, which helps to reduce negative emotional states. This technique can also incorporate spatial anchors for specific states, such as the problem and relevant resources as well as spatial anchors for the orientation in time: past, present, and future.

Here's an example:

Client: Every time I have to stand up for myself, I get anxious and can't do it. Yesterday, my coworker pushed this project on me that I didn't want and shouldn't have to do, but I didn't say anything. People have always been able to walk all over me.

[The emotional nature of the problem indicates that perhaps the right-brain is over-activating.]

Coach: Stand up. [The coach gets the client moving. This helps to engage the left-brain. It also shifts the client's physiology into something that is more engaging.]

Client: What?

Coach: Literally. Stand up. Imagine for a moment a timeline going across the floor. I want you to imagine it going all the way back into your past and all the way forward into your future . . . [The coach begins to set up the spatial anchors for orientation in time. Time becomes a line on the floor.]

Client: OK, I can imagine that.

Coach: Standing in your present . . . Now, take a moment and step back into yesterday . . . Imagine your coworker saying that and notice the feeling you have . . .

Client: Yes, I feel anxious . . . My stomach gets tight . . .

[Moving on the spatial timeline allows the client to re-associate with the feeling.]

Coach: And allow that feeling to take you back in time to another significant moment where you felt it . . . [The coach uses the feeling to begin a regression to cause.]

Client: Yes. [stepping back] This memory of high school just came to me . . . .I didn't speak up when they were bullying my friend, and . . . [The client is delving too deeply back into the negative emotion so the coach does a pattern interrupt . . .]

Coach: Now step off the timeline and see that memory over there . . . From this position, looking at that younger you, what resources do you wish you had had back then? What would you like to give that younger you that would allow her to speak up?

[Stepping off the timeline helps to dissociate the client from the past experience. This dissociation will help the client to find appropriate resources . . .]

Client: Some confidence. Some strength to be able to help my friend and show them I wasn't afraid . . .

Coach: And imagine sending that younger you that confidence now. See her stand a little straighter, taking in that sense of self, strength, and confidence . . .

Client: Yes, I imagine myself standing up and telling them to fuck off and leave her alone. I can see myself taking my friends hand and walking away . . .

Coach: That's right. And as you take a moment to step onto the timeline and into that confident, younger you, walking away with your friend, feeling her hand in yours . . .

[In asking the client to step back onto the timeline, the coach re-associates her into the more resourceful younger version of herself.]

Client: Oh, that feels so much better. [Client smiles, shoulders straighten]

Coach: And I wonder how this might have changed other scenes from your past, if you had that confidence then? [The coach is going to find other memories to change using reconsolidation. The more resourceful state of confidence will be blended with these memories.]

Client: I see myself in college . . . There was an incident . . .

Coach: Step off the timeline . . . [The coach repeats the pattern of dissociation, finding resources, and does a re-association . . .]

Client: Yes, I can imagine sending myself the confidence to say no . . .walk away again . . .

Coach: And as you imagine that you in college, strong, confident, speaking your mind, standing up for yourself, notice what happens.

Client: Yes, it's all different. I can see how that would have changed everything.

Coach: And step into that confidence now. Feel how strong you are as you are walking away from that situation . . . now, allowing yourself to walk confidently on your timeline all the way to yesterday, to that co worker . . .

Client: I imagine myself smiling as I say no, that's not part of my job description, but thank you for offering . . . and I'm definitely going to tell her that tomorrow . . .

Coach: And as you step into tomorrow and imagine seeing her, what are you noticing now? [The coach helps the client to create a future memory]

Client: I tell her, no thanks, and I realize she didn't mean to insult me, she just didn't realize I didn't want to do it . . .

Coach: That's good. Take a few more steps into your future and tell me what comes to you . . .

Client: I feel different. I imagine myself at this wedding I have to go to, and I feel good, like I can talk to anyone.

Coach: Great! And as you look back along your time line, you might notice other things shifting and changing to accommodate this new confidence and realize you have a new foundation to stand on.

When you combine spatial and temporal language, you can really start to move consciousness around. In speaking to a client who has physical pain, we will almost always shift the pain problem into the past along with dissociating from it. This can be accomplished in a number of ways. One is to make statements such as, "That area where that discomfort was . . . " or "That discomfort you've been feeling . . . " or even, "And as you see that sensation over there, what had you been noticing?" In this way you, as coach, can elegantly and seamlessly blend time and space.

These patterns also incorporate language that dissociates, such as "that" versus "this." Take a moment and feel the difference when you look at your hand and say, "This hand here" versus when you say, "That hand there." For most people "that" and "there" move the object subjectively farther away than "this" and "here."

Human beings use the space around them as a metaphorical work area to plan actions and model their world. We have mentioned the work done to discover how the brain codes objects as "near" or "far" (within reach or out of reach) and how this coding changes with the availability of tools that can extend reach. However, there is another branch of exploration that sheds light on just how complex these mental spaces can be.

In particular, researchers, such as Scott Liddell, professor of linguistics at Gallaudet University in Washington DC, have demonstrated how personal space is used literally, symbolically, and metaphorically in sign language. Sign language, of course, uses the same brain territory as spoken language so that it is no great leap to realize that a speaker uses similar spatial reasoning as a signer.

There is actually a whole field of change work that deals with this kind of symbolic space, called "Clean Language." The Clean refers to using language patterns that do not assume, or interfere with, the client's personal spatial map. In Clean Language, nouns and even verbs, whether representing tangible objects or intangibles such as emotions, are all assumed to potentially have a location, which the client is invited to provide. They are also assumed to have object-like characteristics, such as size, shape, color, and so on, again even if they are intangibles.

Within Clean Language, repetition is purposeful because it helps to "fix" the metaphorical landscape in place, as you will notice in the following example:

Client: I am feeling anxious.

Coach: And when you're feeling anxious, where is "anxious"?

Client: Where? Hmm . . . I guess it's here [indicating chest].

Coach: And when "anxious" is there, is that inside or outside?

Client: Inside.

Coach: And when "anxious" is inside, does "anxious" have a size or a shape?

Client: Hmm . . . It's red, like a ball . . . it's vibrating . . .

Coach: And it's red, like a ball, and vibrating, and what do you want to have happen?

Client: I want to feel confident.

Coach: And what kind of "confident" is that "confident"?

Client: [Client shifts posture] It's an energy.

Coach: And where is "confidence," when it's an energy?

Client: It's all over.

Coach: And whereabouts all over?

Client: It surrounds me, like a skin.

Coach: Is there a color of "confident" when it surrounds you like a skin?

Client: Yes, it's gold.

Coach: And when there's "confident," that's energy and it's gold, and it surrounds you like a skin, what happens to "anxious"?

Client: It's gone.

Space as Metaphor

Sometimes movement is implied by shifting perspective. With pain management, we can shift by having the client imagine the pain as a pebble, the pebble on a beach, the beach on an island, the island in an ocean . . . and so on.

We don't know whether that stimulates the hippocampus as well as parts of the visual cortex, but it sure feels like movement in space to us. One day we hope to get our hands, or rather our brains, on a fMRI machine so we can test out our theories. Until then, play with these ideas with an awareness of what is probably happening in the brain and see what happens.

Chapter 11: Identity

When we do change work, we like to make sure to cover all levels of the client's identity, not just the part representing the problem or the part that needs to be different in certain situations, but the client as a whole. This helps the changes to become generative and a natural part of who the client is.

Logical Levels

In NLP, we talk about "logical levels." These cover various aspects of what makes up a person, from the environment in which she lives and acts, her behaviors, feelings, beliefs, and values, all the way up to her identity. Although it's often said that the NLP logical levels are neither logical nor levels, we do believe that, as a general rule, the higher up the logical levels that change is made, the more profound and generative it will be.

So, as coaches, we could help change someone's particular behavior, for example, to stop smoking. This would be a wonderful change for that person, but apart from not smoking and the health effects that come from that, by and large, the person would still be the same person, with the same beliefs, feelings, and values.

In contrast, if we help a client to make a change in the level of identity such as, "I'm a person who loves and respects herself," then the client may stop smoking as a result, but she may also make all sorts of other profound changes in her life. The reason is because this change was made at the level of identity, which is much higher than the level of behavior.

So, who are you in terms of neuroscience? What is your identity? How do you know who you are? In some sense, you don't, at least it's a very hard question to answer. Yet on another level, you do know, do you not?

For example, you are the person who sees what you're seeing, the sensor-of-the-world concept of the self. We use this concept of self as sensor of the world a lot in change work. We say, "See what you're seeing, hear what you're hearing, feel what you're feeling." We associate the person into this particular sensory-sense-of-self. Yet there are a lot more "selves" that you have. You are also the person who makes plans. You can get a client to communicate with this planning-self by asking, "What do you want to work through? How do you want to be different? How will your life be different when you have made this change?" This is the self that has a plan for a person's life. The person is the sensor and also the planner.

Who else might you be? We're talking here in terms of the architecture of the brain. You are oriented in space. You have a spatial orientation that you are aware of. You have a sense of self in the body. The embodied-self.

Consider the questions "Where do you live? How long have you lived there?" For example, we, the authors, have autobiographical selves that know they are living and working in New York City. We can think about our life story. Where were we born? Where did we go to school? We have an autobiographical self that stretches through time.

"How are you feeling now?" That apparent non sequitur was designed to uncover your emotional self. We have an emotional self that tells us how we're feeling at any point in time. Sometimes we're happy, sometimes we're sad, and sometimes we are intensely curious . . .

All these different senses of self are located in different parts of our brain. For example, we could say that the emotional self is the limbic system. Parts of the limbic system have a sense of self, based on how a person is feeling. The autobiographical self is located with memories stored in the sensory portions of the neocortex. Each "self" is different and is stored in different parts of the brain.

There's also a spiritual sense of self. Take a moment and go inside and see if you can get a sense of what some people call their higher self or soul. If that's too religious, think of it as that ineffable sense of self that may be hard to pinpoint but seems to somehow transcend your physical body. For Melissa, this is the totality of her conscious and unconscious self, which she knows she can never fully know. So, there's a spiritual or unknowable self.

We also have the "self as object." Think of yourself as being a human being, flesh and bone. One of seven billion. Think about watching yourself reading this book. This is the self as object.

When we were discussing this with our good friend Mark Simmons, he asked, "What about the self as nonexistent?" That question is very typical of Mark, a Jungian psychologist, and we like that question! That's the negation of the self. I'm not sure where that self is, but Andrew Newberg and two colleagues,

Eugene D'Aquili and Vince Rause, wrote a book called Why God Won't Go Away: Brain Science and the Biology of Belief [New York: Ballantine Books. 2001] that talks about the part of the brain that tells us we are separate from everything else. That part is not fully developed when babies are born. It takes a little bit of time before a baby understands that "this" is her hand and "that" is your hand and that she and you are separate.

Newberg and his coauthors found that—and maybe this is the spiritual self that we're talking about—when people are deep in prayer or meditation, or even whirling like a dervish, the part of the brain that says "I'm a separate self" gets less neural action. How fascinating is that? Think about what the mystics always say: we're all one. We're all connected. So, maybe that's where the nonexistent self is.

Then there's the mirrored self that recognizes you in the mirror. Research suggests that this is a right-brain self. Of course, we also now know about mirror neurons, which you could say are self-as-other, or "me as you." In NLP, we use the concept of perceptual positions to use these concepts of self-as-reflection and self-as-other.

There's also the group self. Current research on the adaptive unconscious lets us know how differently this self acts in a group, especially if you go to a sports event where crowd-mentality can either bring people together or tear them apart based on the color of a sports jersey.

There are so many different types of selves. And again, the cool thing is that all the different parts of the brain have a slightly different sense of self. As you go through these in turn, you begin to activate the different parts of the brain in sequence. This can feel really spacey, but don't take our word for it, simply start to remind yourself in some sequence of your different selves. Give yourself plenty of time to experience each before moving on.

- Notice what you're seeing around you, what you're hearing, what you're sensing about the world around you, your Observer self. Allow yourself time to notice what your sensing self is sensing . . .
- Think about what you're going to do tomorrow or next week or where you going on vacation. The Planner self. Allow yourself time to consider your Planner's plans . . .
- Get a sense of your body in space. Your Embodied self. Allow yourself time to feel your embodied self . . .
- Go back to your childhood, where you went to school, your first job, how you ended up, where you are now. Your Autobiographical self. Allow yourself time to fully recall your Autobiographical self . . .
- Notice how you're feeling. Your Emotional self. Allow yourself time to fully get in touch with your feelings . . .
- Begin to sense your true self, your soul. Allow yourself time to fully meditate on your more expanded self . . .
- Notice everything that you're not, the negation of yourself. Allow yourself no time at all to fully and completely experience everything that you're not.
- Imagine seeing yourself in a mirror. Notice that your reflection is you, the Mirrored self. Allow yourself time to fully reflect on that. Use your mirror neurons to imagine what it would be like to be that person . . .
- Realize that you are part of some larger selves: your family, your business, your circle of friends, your city, your country. Allow yourself time to realize that you are a citizen of the world . . .

How can you use this in your change work? You deal with different selves when you help clients make changes. When you say, "What do you want to work through? How do you want to be different?" you are addressing the client as planner and helping her plan how she wants to change. Maybe the client starts to tell her story. This is the autobiographical self. Changing memories using reconsolidation allows the coach to

233

work with the client's autobiographical self.

Maybe the client becomes emotional during the change work session. This is the emotional self. You can help the client change how she feels about her situation by working with that emotional self.

When you say, "Go back to the time. What are you seeing and hearing?" you are addressing the client as observer. By suggesting that she experiences this in peripheral vision using the foreground-background switch, you can change the observer-self experience.

When you say, "Where do you feel that in your body?" you are addressing the client as the embodied self. By having the client spin the feeling in the opposite direction, you work with the embodied self to help the client change.

Different senses of self are cycled through during change work. You probably do this naturally, but by being more aware that these selves are located in different parts of the brain, will help you be more cognizant of how you are linking and integrating the neurons involved.

You can also use the exercise that follows to move your client through each of these different selves to create a trance that promotes expansion and flexibility. Our ability to help clients become more emotionally and cognitively flexible is one of the keys to generative change. Remember Hebb's Law, which says, neurons that fire together, wire together, so when you cycle through these different selves, you're going to start to wire or connect them up in some way. You're going to create a more integrated self-identity for the client. Isn't that worth investing 10 minutes in the following exercise? It's also a fantastic and fun trance induction.

So, have your client close her eyes as you ask her to

contemplate this series of questions or statements. Give the client plenty of time to consider each statement.

- I would like you to get in touch with your feelings now.
- Notice how you're feeling in your body.
- I would like you to begin to think about why you're here in this office.
- I would like you to imagine seeing yourself in a mirror, seeing your face in the mirror and experience what that's like.
- I would like you to think about your life, where you were born, where you went to school.
- I'd like you to consider the orientation of your body in space.
- I'd like you to imagine seeing yourself coming to this session today, moving through the rest of the population.
- What is your purpose here?
- I'd like you to consider your deeper spiritual self. Who are you in those moments of awe?
- Who are you when you are experiencing joy?
- Who are you when you love?
- See yourself moving into your future with a new story.
- Notice yourself in the mirror having changed what you wanted to change.
- Who are you, now?

Once the client comes out of this experience, let her sit for a bit before sharing feedback. You might be surprised by what he says and who she has discovered herself to be!

Chapter 12: The ACC and Attachment Styles

In Chapter 2, we talked about the work of Dr. Jeffrey Schwartz, and how the brain can become addicted to a problem and work together to maintain and even intensify it. Fortunately, it is not all doom and gloom in Dr. Schwartz's world, and he lists several friends and allies in the quest for a better life. These include the wise advocate, which is the part of you that understands, loves, and cares about you both physically and emotionally.

Dr. Schwartz does not suggest a specific neuroscience mechanism for the wise advocate, but a lot of other research supports this concept. This leads us to one of our favorite parts of the brain. Shawn used to say it was his favorite part until his visual cortex got pissed off about it. So, now, he says it is just one of his favorite parts of the brain, the anterior cingulate cortex or the ACC.

The ACC sits between the PFC and the limbic system, which is your emotional brain. The ACC also reaches up to your motor cortex on top so it links to action, thought and emotion. It can connect to pretty much everything that makes you who you are.

In the ACC are neurons called spindle cells that are long and thin, like a spindle. These cells only exist in human beings, great apes, whales, and dolphins, and, as recently discovered, in elephants. Researchers believe these spindle cells are linked to social interactions that are only available to species that live in close social groups. These cells are also called Von Economo cells, after the man who first described them in 1926.

The spindle cells also are found in the frontal insula, which is associated with empathy. Look around and find another person. Look at the person's face and begin to empathize with his or her feelings. Really feel what the person may be feeling and intending to do. As you do that, you are lighting up your frontal insula.

A key element in terms of changing into who you want to be is to care about yourself. The ability to love and care about yourself and others may be related to spindle cells. Being forgiving of yourself and others has been shown to strengthen the parts of the brain, including the ACC and insula, associated with compassion.

Exercise: Strengthening the ACC

Doing the following exercise with your clients will develop and strengthen their ACC and help them to have more compassion for themselves. It is a three-step exercise:

Step one: Associate the client into a time when she felt loved and cared for with the following words:

"'Associate' means to get in touch with the feeling of, 'I feel loved and cared for.' Think of a time when you felt totally loved and cared for. Go back to that time. See what you're seeing, hear what you're hearing, and feel what you're feeling. Maybe imagine a time where you were a child and felt totally loved and cared for by your mother or grandmother. Whenever it was, go back to that time and feel loved and cared for."

Step two: Associate the client into a time when she felt totally loving and caring toward someone else, perhaps a child. Wording would be as follows:

"Remember a time when you felt totally loving and caring toward someone, maybe for your child or a nephew or niece or perhaps even a pet. Go back to that time. See what you're seeing, hear what you're hearing, and feel what you're feeling."

Through practice of the first two steps, the client has the experience of being loved and cared for and of loving and caring for another person.

Step three: Associate the client into the other person visualized in step 1 and then into the other person visualized in step 2. Wording would be as follows:

"Float into that other person and fully experience feeling loved and cared for by yourself. So, if the person who you feel loved and cared for in step one is your mother, float in and become your mother, and love and care for yourself as a child. Similarly, if the person who you care about in step two is your child, then imagine floating into your child and feeling that sense of love from yourself."

Mixing these perceptual positions and giving and receiving a sense of love from each of these perceptual positions strengthens the ACC.

Grief

One way of thinking about grief is, "I know what it's like to be loved and cared for by another person, and now that person is gone." The power of loving and caring for yourself is that you don't leave yourself. You don't break up with yourself so you can always be there for you, as long as you know how to love yourself.

Sometimes a client will say that she has never felt loved or has never loved someone else. Using some of the other processes in this book to help reframe or change semantic memory will make it easier for such a client to do this exercise. That being said, perhaps the client has loved a pet or has seen a movie that encapsulated loving feelings. Experiencing feelings of love and being loved will strengthen the ACC no matter how they are accessed.

ACC and Attachment Theory

The ACC plays a big role in attachment theory, which explains how the way a child is treated while growing up creates an attachment style that has an impact on the rest of her lives. If a child grows up in an environment in which she is loved, cared for and supported, then she will likely have a very positive and healthy attachment style. If she doesn't experience this growing up, it may cause many different problems later in life. This can be rewired and changed, though.

Amazing work is being done in this area. A great book by Bonnie Badenoch called Being a Brain-Wise Therapist: A Practical Guide to Interpersonal Neurobiology [New York: W. W. Norton & Company. 2008] discusses bringing knowledge of the brain into therapy. When she's working with someone who does not have a positive attachment style, she relaxes into a heart centered, compassionate state that the client's brain can mirror. In this way, when the client talks about painful experiences or trauma, a warm, loving space is created by Badenoch to support the client. It's as if Badenoch is utilizing reconsolidation to add an element of safety that the client never had while growing up. She can access the wise advocate for herself and imagine it holding the client. She considers this holding a right-brain state for the client.

Milton Erickson dealt with this issue in his book The February Man: Evolving Consciousness and Identity in Hypnotherapy [New York; Taylor & Francis Group. 1989]. He was working with a client who may have had some kind of attachment disorder. This client had had a lonely childhood, having been abandoned by her father, and having a mother who had to work to support the family. Erickson would put her in trance, regress her to childhood, and appear as a wise uncle at different pivotal moments throughout her life so that she could get an experience of positive, loving support while growing up. He created a foundation of experience for the client of what it's like to be absolutely cared for.

The ACC affects our ability to form healthy attachments because it touches the rational, emotional, and action parts of the brain. Think of it this way, if you decide to hug a person because you like him or her, that's your ACC, linking those three parts. You've thought about an action based on an emotion.

Of course, if your client is in a negative emotional state (which she may well be when she comes to see you), her lack of feeling loved could simply be attributed to the state she is in. Remember, state-dependent learning means that the brain is filtering for like-minded emotional states. Therefore, you need to do a pattern interrupt and associate the client into a positive state. If after doing so the client still says, "You know, I've never been loved," then it would be worthwhile to spend a session that takes her through this exercise and increases the power of her ACC.

Compassion Exercise

Rick Hansen in his book Buddha's Brain: The Practical Neuroscience of Happiness, Love, and Wisdom [Oakland, CA: New Harbinger Publications. 2009], describes a simple yet powerful compassion meditation in which a person gets into a relaxed state and thinks of someone she loves and feels gratitude and compassionate for, then thinks of a stranger and extends this gratitude and compassion to that person. Then, the meditator thinks of someone she dislikes and extends gratitude and compassion to that person, and, finally, the meditator extends compassion and gratitude to herself.

We teach our clients to access a heart-centered space before doing this or similar exercises. There is a lot of interesting research coming out of the Heart Math Institute that suggests focusing on the heart to generate different brain wave states. We suggest spending some time looking into this work. A good place to start is heartmath.com.

Heart Breathing Exercise:

Sit comfortably and close your eyes. Focus your attention on the area around your heart and imagine you can breath through it. Imagine, in whatever way is comfortable, that you can see or feel the energy moving through your heart as you breathe. When your mind wanders, gently bring it back to your heart and breathe.

As you're heart-breathing, think of someone you care about and imagine sending that love, from your heart, to that person. Imagine that love streaming from your heart, wrapping around the person, and then imagine breathing it back in, creating a loop, a connection, of love."

We find that many clients find it easier to send love to a child or pet than to feel compassion for themselves. This exercise allows them to breathe in the unconditional love they feel for someone else, and it usually provides the emotional state needed to begin to feel more love and forgiveness for themselves.

Meditation and mindfulness training also have been shown to have measurable positive effects on the brain in relation to strengthening compassion and the ACC. Cultivating compassion is just one of the many benefits of mindfulness meditation. The practice also has been shown to strengthen attention and focusing abilities while tempering emotional reactivity.

A study led by Sara Lazar, a researcher at the Massachusetts General Hospital in Boston, showed that just 8 weeks of mindfulness meditation caused structural changes in the brain. She found an increase in grey-matter density in the hippocampus, which is associated with learning and memory, and in areas associated with compassion and self-awareness. It also showed a decrease in grey-matter density in the amygdala, which as we discussed, plays a pivotal role in stress and anxiety.

This is exciting news because it shows that you don't have to be a devoted, long-time meditator to reap the brain benefits.

As a matter of fact, people who are not so good at quieting the mind and are constantly waging an inner battle to focus on their breath during meditation are actually strengthening the areas in the brain associated with will power. In the book, The Willpower Instinct: How Self-Control Works, Why It Matters, and What You Can Do To Get More of It [New York: Avery. 2012], author Kelly McGonal likens this inner struggle to flexing the muscles needed to improve focus, concentration, and motivation. So, instead of being discouraged by the wandering mind, you can think of each instance as a great brain workout. How cool is that? You don't need to devote half your life to this practice. Even 10 minutes a day has been proven to result in wonderful changes in the brain.

Chapter 13: Libet and Unconscious Influence

Dr. Jeffrey Schwartz work is based, in part, on some of the research produced by Benjamin Libet (1916-2007), whose experiments challenge our concept of free will and self determinism. The question of free will has been a topic of philosophical debate for centuries. Some philosophers argue that immediately following the Big Bang, the movement of every atom in the universe was determined from then until eternity, like a giant clock. Other philosophers argue that the Blind Watchmaker must have provided us with free will because, without it, how could we choose right from wrong?

As a philosophical matter, this appears to be beyond the competence of science to resolve. However, Libet's experiments in the 1980s showed that there may not be such a thing as free will within the human experience, at least not in the way we think of it.

Libet asked subjects to look at a giant clock face with a very rapidly turning hand while holding their fingers over a button. Watching the clock-hand turn allowed the subjects to judge time with great accuracy. Libet asked them to watch the second hand turn, and, at some point, make a conscious decision to press the button and immediately do so as soon as they had consciously made the decision. The subjects were, therefore, able to subjectively report the exact time when they made the conscious decision to press the button.

The button itself was attached to a second time measurement device, which measured the exact instant the button was pressed. Not surprisingly, Libet found that the decision to press the button preceded the actual pressing of the button by the fraction of a second it took the subject's finger to descend.

Libet's genius, however, lay in the third measurement of time. You see, Libet also wired the subjects' brains up to a scanner designed to measure the response potential in their motor cortices. This effectively captured the moment in time when the subjects' motor cortices prepared to move the subjects' hand down to the button.

Now, you would expect that the sequence of events would be as follows: consciously make a decision to press the button, response potential builds in the motor cortex, hand moves down and presses button.

Libet found that the conscious decision to take an action happened after the firing of the neurons in the brain prepared for that action. How could this be? Libet speculated that the brain was tricking the conscious mind into believing that it had decided to take the action. In fact, the decision was made unconsciously.

Why do we do that? What's the benefit of getting ourselves ahead of our decision? We're just guessing here, but making the decision unconsciously is much faster and far more informed. The unconscious, as we've already discussed, is capable of multisensory processing at a scale that the conscious mind cannot even imagine. It's probably a holdover from when our ancestors needed to get away from those raptors quickly. We, as hypnotists, understand the primacy of the adaptive unconscious and are not under the impression that all we are is what our conscious mind is aware of. So, this research doesn't necessarily lead us to the conclusion that we don't have free will, just that "we" is a much bigger concept than the conscious mind can imagine.

But, as a species, we seem to need the illusion of conscious decision-making to keep our sense of conscious control. What is fascinating about the adaptive unconscious is that it has many cognitive filters and biases that prop up our sense of self. We tell ourselves stories that justify things we do and decisions we make when, in reality, our processing and motivations are, for the most part, completely out of our conscious awareness. This allows us to feel in control because, if there's one thing the conscious mind abhors, its uncertainty. We have been known, as a species, to grasp at any explanation to soothe the discomfort of uncertainty, and the brain is constantly filling in gaps and creating illusions to keep this sense of cohesion in place.

Try this experiment: Look at your hands while you clap. Listen for the sound, feel the clap, and see your hands touch. Do these actions take place at the same time? In fact, the answer is no because light, sound, and nerve impulses travel at different speeds, but it is as if they move simultaneously because your brain wants you to experience the world in a way that makes sense. It doesn't want you to see something and then hear the sound it makes later. It's a comfort-thing.

We can't reproduce Libet's experiment here, but we can let you feel the effect. You'll need to write this down, so pick up a pen; no, actually, pick up a cup instead. You'll notice that, if you offer someone a pen, she will reach for the pen as if about to write, using the motor program associated with writing. The person will generally reach for a cup with a hand opened in the shape of a cup, as if the person were going to drink. The relevant motor program is being loaded onto the person's motor cortex before a decision to take the action has been made. This why guys on the street snap out a flyer before they say, "Do you want the flyer?" After you've taken the flyer, you ask yourself "Why the heck did I take that? What do I do with this now?" This is your unconscious making decisions for you.

Anyway, as a result of his experiment, Libet showed that there was no such thing as free will, at least not on a conscious basis. Fortunately for those of us who believe in and consciously value free will, Libet identified a small escape clause. He found that the conscious mind had the ability to veto any action that had been decided on by the unconscious mind. "Free will" became "Free won't"!

So, even if your brain has loaded and started the motor program to take the flyer, you can cancel it. Many times, while walking to work, Shawn's hand makes a move to reach for the flyer, and he stops it and says, "No thanks," or Melissa stops herself from reaching for another cookie even though her hand has already moved toward the plate.

In the context of OCD and other compulsions, this means that, while the compulsion may begin unconsciously, the conscious mind does indeed have the ability to stop the behavior. This is the principle on which Dr. Schwartz based his treatment.

Another interesting set of studies involves a tool called the Columbia Card Task (CCT) and shows the importance of unconscious foreknowledge in decision-making. In a typical CCT test, the subject is given two to four decks of cards, which are loaded to make someone either lose money, or make money, but in such a way that it is not obvious which are the losing decks and which the winning decks.

The CCT is used to test to what extent subjects evaluate risk on a cognitive or emotional level and how this varies over different age ranges, cultural backgrounds, and so on. We are interested in it because it shows, in principle, that the unconscious, emotional mind is heavily involved in decision-making.

In using the CCT, researchers observe when the subjects start to play with the winning deck. They also ask the subjects when they know which deck they should play with and how they know. They also measure skin conductivity to gauge emotional arousal as a card game is played. After a few rounds, the subjects will begin playing with the winning deck, even though they will claim that they don't consciously know which deck is the winning deck. It takes many additional rounds before the conscious mind catches up and says, "This deck is the one I prefer."

Even more interestingly, three minds are evaluating the decisions. They're asking the person playing the game, "What's going on? What's the best deck?" and the subject says, "I don't know," even though her brain has already figured it out. But even before the subject's unconscious mind starts choosing correctly, she sweats and her skin conductivity goes down when she reaches for the wrong deck. So, her body knows first, her unconscious mind knows second, and her conscious mind knows last. It's true that a person's hands are smarter than her head, at least sometimes, anyway.

Coaching Metaphor

Libet proved that your conscious mind rarely decides to do anything. It doesn't decide to smoke a cigarette or eat a doughnut because the decision is made by your unconscious mind according to a set of rules that you are not even consciously aware of. What's important is that, with your "free-won't," you can decide not to smoke that cigarette or eat that doughnut. All you have to do is to make a decision . . . not to.

Throughout this book, we offer many different techniques and processes that exercise the "free won't" to make it easier to change those unconscious patterns. This will create a deeper connection between the conscious and unconscious mind making change even easier over time.

Chapter 14: Conclusion: Putting the Brain into Coaching

We have introduced you to some interesting concepts of neuroscience, and we hope we've stimulated areas of your brain enough to inspire you to do the same for your clients. All that remains is to offer some final thoughts on taking these principles off of the page and into your practice.

Neuroscience has come along way over the past 25 years. Through neuroscientific research, we now have a complete map of a mouse's brain, and futurists, including the great Stephen Hawking, speculate that within 30 years, you will be able to download a copy of your brain onto the hard drive of your computer! While we cannot vouch for this last speculation, it is certainly true that absorbing just a fraction of the current brain research will provide you with valuable tools and ideas for your practice. After all, neuroscience provides a limitless supply of metaphors for why a client should interrupt her old, negative patterns and how she can install new ways of thinking to literally change the wiring of the brain.

One of the most amazing and powerful things to know about your brain is that it can rewire itself and can do so within an instant. People expect change to be long and difficult, but by understanding the principles of LTP and Hebb's Law, you can explain how rapid change can actually be. This book has provided many ways for you to communicate this to your clients in a way that will allow them to believe in and embrace that rapid change.

Now, while change can take place in an instant, lasting change requires that your clients remember new ways of thinking and feeling and forget those old patterns that no longer serve them. Having learned how the different types of memory work, you can help your clients to do this in many creative ways. Sharing how the brain reconsolidates memories opens up your change work for new and exciting interventions.

You can help clients use their working memory to run movies with soundtracks and positive titles of how they want to be that support and reinforce the changes while promoting new neural connections. When they lock these positive movies in place using good dopamine for full attention density, these new patterns begin to be automatically transferred into long-term memory.

Forgetting the old ways of being takes a little more work; after all, we do not have free will, but we do have free won't and the ability to say no to thoughts and feelings that no longer serve us. As a coach, therapist, or hypnotist, you can teach your clients to use this veto power by providing them with the tools to interrupt their own patterns. Techniques such as EFT, peripheral vision, heart breathing and bilateral stimulation arm your clients with powerful ways to change emotional states so that breaking patterns is easier. When your clients learn these tools, they will truly understand the meaning of self-directed neuron plasticity.

In addition to these general principles of change, we have given you a glimpse of some of the more interesting areas of your brain, such as your visual cortex, amygdala, ACC, and others. Holding in mind even a simple map of how the brain works will allow you to explain to your clients why and how the work you are doing together will help them change. It gives them a reason to follow your suggestions and do the homework.

Of course, change work does not take place just within your brain or within the brain of a client. It takes place in the space in between you and your client, a space that is influenced by neural processes governed by mirror neurons and spindle cells. These processes will lead to a deeper level of rapport between coach and client, and all you, as a change worker, have to do is relax and let these processes do their job.

Finally, we hope this book has inspired you to bring creativity, play, and huge doses of dopamine into your sessions. We imagine that having a better idea of what's going on under the hood will excite your neurons with possibilities for years to come. After all, we are all on a journey of self-discovery! Bon voyage!

About the Authors:

Melissa Tiers is the founder of The Center for Integrative Hypnosis with a private practice in New York City. She is an international lecturer, trainer and award-winning author, who teaches clinical hypnosis, NLP, and mental health coaching to practitioners from all over the world. Melissa is an adjunct faculty member of The New York Open Center and The Tri-State College of Acupuncture where she teaches classes in mind/body medicine.

The Center for Integrative Hypnosis is located at 135 west 29th street, suite 604 and offers a variety of workshops, seminars, and certification trainings. Melissa also has an online video training site that features some of her most popular courses. For more information go to www.centerforintegrativehypnosis.com or www.melissatiers.com
Other books by this author include:

Integrative Hypnosis: A Comprehensive Course in Change
The Anti-Anxiety Toolkit: Rapid Techniques to Rewire your Brain

Originally from England, Shawn Carson is co-founder of the International Center for Positive Change and Hypnosis in New York City. He is an international consultant, trainer, coach, hypnotist and author.

Shawn teaches with his partners Sarah Carson and Jess Marion at International Center for Positive Change and Hypnosis is located at 545 8th Avenue, Suite 930 and offer NLP and hypnosis certifications, as well as workshops on subjects as diverse as past life regression, the anthropology of trance, NLP for business and deep trance identification (DTI). For more information go to BestNLPNewYork.com, or ChangingMindPublishing.com.

Other books by this author include:

QUIT: The hypnotists handbook to running effective stop smoking sessions (with Sarah Carson and Jess Marion)

The Swish, Part of the NLP Mastery Series (with Jess Marion)

The Visual Squash, Part of the NLP Mastery Series (with Jess Marion)

Upcoming titles include:

Deep Trance Identification (with Jess Marion and John Overdurf)

Index

A

ACC. *See* Anterior cingulate cortex
Adaptive unconscious, 246
Affect regulation, 39, 41
Alpha brainwave pattern, 139, 140
Amygdala, 170
  danger signals from, 174
  "fight or flight" response, 171
  freeze response, 171–172
  "low road" to, 170–171
Amygdala hijacks, 142
  causes of, 174
  V-K dissociation pattern for
    client example of, 175–179
    submodality shifts, 174
"Anchor"
  consequences for setting, 19
  definition of, 18
  emotional response, 19
  intensity and repetition, 19
Anterior cingulate cortex
  and attachment theory
    growing up child, 239
    healthy attachments, 240
    reconsolidation, 239–240
  functions of, 34
  location of, 236–237
  meditation and mindfulness training
    effect on, 242
  spindle cells in, 237
  strengthening exercise, 237–238
Antidepressant drugs and brain function,
    32
Anxiety, 191–193
  and negative experience, 108
  performance, 116
  sensory experience of, 86–87
Attention
  and dopamine, 58–59
  importance in learning, 93
  and learning, 159–160
  types of, 93
  ways to achieve, 93–95
  to working memory, 95–96

Attention density, 88–89, 91
  and attention, 93–95
  and bodily sensation, 97–99
  and emotional attention, 96–'
  increased using repetition, 99
  reinforcing change with, 99–'
  and repetition, 92
  and working memory, 95–96
Auditory anchor, 18
Auditory cortex, 17
Auditory submodalities, 85

B

"Background," 137
Basal ganglia
  components of, 35
  functions of, 35
"Be here now" concept, 143
Beliefs and values as implicit
    125–126
Bilateral stimulation
  applications of, 191
  as pattern interrupt, 191–194
Blended space, 218
Blind spot, experiencing, 135–13(
Bodily sensation
  associating into, 97–99
  dissociating from, 99
Body language, 133
Bottom-up learning, 117
Brain, 12. *See also* Hemispheres o:
  addiction to problem, 160–1(
  anterior cingulate cortex. *Se*
    cingulate cortex
  and blind spot, 135–136
  blood flow to, 194
  flexibility in, 39
  function changes using placel
  mind as "epiphenomenon" o
  physical structure of, 30
  potential connections within,
  purpose of, 63–64
  rewiring of, 46

space-time metaphors. *See* Space-time metaphors

stress response, 65–66

tendency to generalize, 28–29

   and depressed state, 29

   and emotional state, 29

   and links to problems, 28–29

visual processing. *See* Visual processing

Brain activity, 31, 41

   and emotional words, 47–48

   generalizations about, 185–187

   left-brain, 184–185, 197

   right-brain, 187

Brain areas, 45

   activated by language and gestures, 213–214

   amygdala, 34

   anterior cingulate cortex, 34

   Assessment Center, 36–38

      activity in, 41, 45–46

   damage to, 13–14

   functions of, 34

   Habit Center, 35

   insula, 34

   Reward Center, 35

   Self-Referencing Center, 35–36

   "Uh-Oh Center" of, 34, 35

      activity in, 41

Brain injury, effect of, 13–14

Brain map, 164–167

Brain mapping using live human subjects, 14

Brain research

   history of, 12

      Aristotle's view, 13

      brain mapping using live human subjects, 14

      damage to brain areas, 13–14

      Galen's view, 13

      hippocampus, 14

      localized memory, 106–107

      Pharaohs, 13

      split-brain experiments, 14

     scanning techniques and, 14–15

Brain surgery in children, 16

Broca's area, 14, 183

Buddhist monks, neuroplastic effects of meditation on brains of, 31

C

"Canonical neuron," 129

CCT. *See* Columbia Card Task

Cerebral cortex, 34

Change Personal History patterns, 67

   memory reconsolidation using, 72–78

   in terms of accessed memories, 81–82

Change work, 47, 170, 252

   changing behavior, 229–230

   in cognitive way, 79

   conversation-based, 72–79

   focused or phasic attention. *See* Focused or phasic attention

   generating new experiences in clients during, 66–67

   humor and curiosity usage during, 90

   hypnosis, 78–80

   identity usage in, 233–234

   intrinsic attention. *See* Intrinsic attention

   linking with client's life, 100–101

   long-term memory formation, 87–90

   open loop related to, 105

   permanent, 62

   reinforcing, 79

   and trance, 78–79

   weight of science behind, 62

Clean Language, 227

Client's state, calibration of, 29

Clients' stories. *See* Problem, emotional or behavioral

Coaching

   addiction or compulsion in context of, 158–159

   brain activity, left–right–left–right, 185

   client's attention to new information, 136–137

   emotion labeling, 41–42

   gestures and client's unconscious mind, 214–215

   long-term memory formation application to, 104–105

   new behavior, 59–60

   Schwartz's protocol to, 38–40

   working memory usage in, 59–62

Coaching pattern

   associate into problem, 49–50

   associate into resource, 50

   dissociate from problem, 50

example of, 50–54
resource and problem, collapse of, 50
Columbia Card Task, 247–248
Compassion exercise, 240–241
Compulsion, 247
Conscious
awareness, 246
decision-making, illusion of, 246
Conscious mind, 79, 187
problem and left-brain, 188
to take action, 245
Conscious-unconscious dissociation, 189
Context-dependent memory, 219–220
"Context reframe," 85
Conversation-based change work, 72–79
Corpus callosum, 182
Cultural differences and space-time metaphors, 222

D
Deceptive brain message
concept of, 161–162
definition of, 161
examples of, 161
gambling and dopamine rush, 166–167
identification of, 43
negative behaviors with, 162, 165
pre-framing client about, 166
recovery strategies, 167
reframing, 166
steps to deal with, 162–163
"Disney Strategy" pattern, 220–221
Dissociation, 29
Dopamine, 156, 251
and client's attention, 58–59
function of, 57–58
and learning, 159–160
and "reward circuit," 157
Dopamine crash, 158
Dopamine rush
activities creating, 157–158
and gambling, 166

E
Elevators, fear of, 29
Embodied self, 234
Emotional attention and attention density,
96–97
Emotional impact of incidents
anxiety issues, 65–66
changing, 66–67
Emotional label of memory, 82
Emotional response
and Assessment Center, 41, 4
regulating, 41
Emotional self, 231, 234
Emotional words and brain activi
Emotions, 170
labeling, 40–42
Empathy and mirror neurons, 13
Environments, mental and ph
effects of, 217–218
Episodic memory, 56, 80
changed in positive way, 113
Change Personal History pat
82
definition of, 65
formation of, 88
Ericksonian hypnosis technique,
Error-detection circuit, 165
Executive brain. See Frontal corte
Expectation and hope, 163
Experience-dependent neuroplas
definition of, 31
importance of, 32
Eyes
fovea, 134–135
optic nerve of, 134
retina of, 134
as sense organs, 134

F
"False brain messages," 38
"Fight or flight" response, 171
Flashbulb memory, emotionality
Focused or phasic attention
and intrinsic attention, 94–95
need for creating state of, 93-
"Foreground," 137
Foreground-background switch,
Forgetting, emotional experienc
118
Forgetting-power of positive
115–116
Foveal vision, 134–135, 137, 139

focusing in, 139
and peripheral vision, switch between, 137
Free will
Libet's experiments on, 244–245, 247
and unconscious decision making, 245–247
Freeze response, 171–172
Frontal cortex, 35
Frontal insula, spindle cells in, 237
"Future memory," 65

G
Gage, Phineas, 13
Gambling and dopamine rush, 166
Generalization
about brain function, 185–187
and memory integration, 109–110
Gestures
calibrating to, 215–216
influence on client's unconscious mind, 214–215
and language, 212
brain areas activated by, 213–214
Goal setting, 211–212
Gratification, delayed, 43–44
Grief, 239
Grieving, 168
Group self, 232

H
Heart breathing exercise, 241–242
Hebb's Law, 15, 30, 251
brain rewiring mechanism, 16–17
examples in practice, 17–18
and long-term potentiation
anchoring, 18–22
neuron wiring mechanism, 18
Pavlov's views on, 16
process of generalization, 28
and stimulus-driven neurons, 16–17
Hemispheres of brain. See also Left-brain; Right-brain
corpus callosum, 182
explanations for, 182–183
left hemisphere. See Left hemisphere
misinformation about, 181

right hemisphere. See Right hemisphere
Sperry's early research on, 182
switching between
bilateral stimulation exercise for, 191–194
bilateral stimulation for, 191
doing math, 184
inductive language patterns, 190
left-brain/right-brain preferences, 185–187
trance induction, 184
Hemispheric disagreement, 195, 196
Hidden ability pattern, 114–115
Hidden commands and suggestions, priming effects of, 124
Hippocampus, 14, 57–58
and dopamine, 159
role in context-dependent memory, 220
role in memory formation and storage, 89–90, 103–104
and stress, 172
fear of flying, 173
generalization, 172–173
memory with mouse, 174
HNLP meta-pattern
definition of, 44
importance of, 47
in office setting, 47
in practice, 48–49
steps of, 44
associate into problem, 45, 48
associate into resource, 46, 49
dissociate from problem, 45–46, 48–49
resource and problem, collapse of, 46, 49
Hope and expectation, 163
Humanistic Neuro Linguistic Programming (HNLP) meta-pattern. See HNLP meta-pattern
Hypnosis
change work through, 78–80
interspersal technique and priming, 123–125

I
Identity

and self. *See* Self
in terms of neuroscience, 230
usage in change work, 233–234
work for changing level of, 230
Implicit memories, 81
beliefs and values as, 125–126
definition of, 119
formation of, 119–120
Inferior frontal regions, activation of, 213–214
Inner state management, 132
Insula (insular cortex), 34
Intrinsic attention, 137
definition of, 93
ways to achieve, 94–95
to working memory, 95–96

K
Kinesthetic anchor, 18
Kinesthetic submodalities, 85

L
Labeling
problem, 43
thoughts and emotions, 40–42, 45–46
Lama, Dalai
on mind and brain, 31
Landscapes
learning, 206–207
physical movement and mental, combining, 222–226
Language
and gestures, 212–214
brain areas activated by, 213–214
processing, 190
Learning
and attention, 159–160
and dopamine, 159–160
and sleep, 103–104
ways of, 117
Learning circuit
dopamine release, 57–58
paying attention, 58–59
Learning patterns, 105
Left-brain, 186
functions of, 183
preferences of, 187–188

and right-brain, differences 186–187
and right-brain phrases,
between, 189
and right-brain, structural c
between, 183–184
Left-brain/right-brain preferenc
187
balance using visual squash,
See also Visual squa:
conscious–unconscious d
pattern in, 188
Left-brain stroke, 186
Left hemisphere, 181
Limbic system, 97
amygdala. *See* Amygdala
functions of, 172
sense of self, 231
Logical levels, 229
Long-term memory, 62, 87, 251
definition of, 88
formation during change woi
coaching for, 104–105
episodic memory, 88
hippocampus, 89–90
and sleep, 103–104
steps of, 91–93
working memory, 88–89
memory reconsolidation. *Se*
reconsolidation
Long-term potentiation, 31, 251
anchoring process, 18–22
consequences for setting,
examples, 19–22
external stimulus, 18
state of confidence, 19–2
neuron wiring mechanism, 1£
and Quantum Zeno effect,
between, 24
temporary sensitivity, 24
Loss and mourning, 168
LTP. *See* Long-term potentiation

M
Manic-depression, 195
Map-across technique of NLP
information coding and subi
144–145

internal representations, differences
between
    examples, 146–147
    in visual cortex, 145–146
    memory and visual cortex, 145–147
"Meaning reframe" intervention, 84
Meditation
    and mindfulness training, 242
    neuroplastic effects of, 31
Memory
    emotional label of, 82
    formation of, 88–90
    importance in change work, 56
    localized, research on, 106–107
    reframing of, 83–84
    types of, 56, 80–81
        overlapping of, 81
Memory distribution
    definition of, 106
    negative experiences, 107–108
    Penfield's work on, 106–107
    positive experiences, 108–109
    and sensory access points, 107
Memory extinction, 112
    change in episodic memories with, 113
    forgetting through, 114
    research on, 113
Memory formation, mechanics of, 65–66
Memory integration
    definition of, 106, 109
    and generalization, 109–110
    and positive neural networks, 109–110
Memory of space, storage of, 140
Memory reconsolidation
    change in episodic memories with, 113
    definition of, 67–68, 106, 111
    and extinction, 112
    importance of understanding, 68
    and pattern interrupts, 112–114
    positive and negative issues, 112
    research on, 68–70, 113
    using Change Personal History pattern,
        72–78
    using re-imprinting, 70–71
Mental representation, 17
Mind
    changing, 33
    as "epiphenomenon" of brain, 30
    impact on brain physical structure, 30

Mindfulness. See Intrinsic attention
"15 minute rule," 43
Mirror neurons
    discovery of, 128
    and empathy, 130
    exercising, 131–132
    firing of, 129–130
    functions of, 127–128
    ideas about, 127
    implications of
        building rapport with clients, 130–
            132
        pattern interrupt, 132
        state of confidence in client, 131
    response to sounds, 129
    and sporting event, 128–129
Motive, purpose of, 63–64
Movement
    shifting perspective, 228
    and space. See Space and movement,
        metaphors of

N
"Near" and "far" concept
    and brain, link between, 207–208
    with NLP submodalities, 208–211
        demonstration of, 210–211
        picture of person/location, 208–
            210
Negative behaviors, 43
    and deceptive brain message, 162
Negative emotion, 34
Negative experiences, 107–108
Negative feeling, 43
Neural connections and long-term
    memory, 27
"Neural Correlates of Consciousness," 30
Neural-Darwinism, 167–168
Neural networks, 23, 25–26, 39, 46–47
    linking problem to positive, 110–111
    transformation of, 46–47
Neurogenesis, 15
Neuromodulators
    dopamine, 156
    norepinephrine, 156
    serotonin, 156
Neuronal link, reactions reinforcing, 34
Neuron pruning

definition of, 114
ways to promote
  forgetting, 115–116
  hidden ability pattern, 114–115
  recovery strategy, 116–117
Neurons, 16
  connections within, 12–13, 18
  firing and neurotransmitters, 18
  sensitivity for firing, 156
Neuroplasticity, 140
Neuroscience, 250
Neurotransmitters, 18
  definition of, 154
  discovery of, 154–155
  functions of, 155
  gamma-aminobutyric acid, 156
  glutamate, 155–156
  in "reward circuit," 157
New behavior
  coaching, 59–60
  and repetition, 62
NLP
  "Disney Strategy" pattern, 220–221
  logical levels in. See Logical levels
  Perfect Parents pattern, 701–72
  visual squash. See Visual squash
  What and Where pathway usage in
    map-across technique, 144–148
    Swish pattern technique, 148–152
Non-REM sleep, memory formation
  during, 104
Nonverbal communication
  congruent with emotional states, 131–
    132
  importance for coach, 133
Norepinephrine, 156

O
Obsessive-compulsive disorder, 34
  brain processes involved in, 34
  and dopamine rush, 164–165
  OCD thoughts, 37
OCD. See Obsessive-compulsive disorder
Old behavior, reevaluation of, 46–47
Open focus. See Peripheral vision
Open-focus exercise, 141

P
Parasympathetic nervous system,
  activation of, 137, 194
Pattern interrupts, 29, 39, 100, 11
  bilateral stimulation as, 191–1
  and memory reconsolidation,
  mirror neurons, 132
  open-focus exercise as, 139, 1
Penfield, Wilder, 16
  brain mapping using liv
    subjects, 14
Perfect Parents pattern, 701–72
Performance anxiety, 116
Peripheral vision, 135
  advantages of
    blending of foveal and
      states, 138–139
  alpha brainwave pattern, 139
  exercise using, 139, 141
  flexibility with, 139–140
  lead your client into, 138
Peripheral visual field, 135
Personal space, 226
PFC. See Prefrontal cortex
Phasic attention, 137
Phobias, 83, 108, 174
  development of, 28
Physical movement and mental
  combining, 222–226
Placebo effect, 47
  on brain function, 32
Positive experiences, 107–109.
  Memory reconsolidatio
  and memory reconsolidation,
Positive neural networks, 27
  and memory integration, 109
Positive thought, forgetting-p
  115–116
Posterior temporal regions, acti
  213–214
Posthypnotic suggestions, 105, 1
Postsynaptic neuron, 155
Post-traumatic stress disorder
  symptoms, 83
Prefrontal cortex, 35–36, 97, 117
  as Assessment Center, 36
  functions of, 42
  "high road" to, 170
  message to amygdala, 171

role in context-dependent memory, 220
"top-down processing," 42–43
Presynaptic neuron, 155
Priming, 120–123
  examples of, 120–121
  experiments on
    pre-talk sets up, 122
    scrambled sentence quiz, 121–122
    word search puzzles, 121
  factors influencing, 123
  using intake form with questions, 123
  using interspersal technique, 123
    hidden commands and suggestions, 124
    metaphors, 124–125
    pre-frames, 125
  using objects associated with business, 123
  verbal or nonverbal, 120
Problem, emotional or behavioral, 12
  attention density impact on, 100
  dissociating client from, 45–46
  emotional reactivity to, 137
  links and associations on, 28–29
  and recovery strategies, 116
  resource in context of, 46
  solution of, 136–137
  stabilizing, 25–26, 39
  unwanted feeling, 137
  ways to get rid of
    absence of audience, 26–27
    HNLP meta-pattern. *See* HNLP meta-pattern
    pattern interrupts, 26
Procedural memory, 56
Psychological problems and hemispheric disagreement, 195
Psychotherapy, 27

Q
Quantum Zeno effect, 33, 136
  application to neural networks, 35
  and LTP, difference between, 24
  as metaphor of neuroplasticity, 27
  pattern interrupts to break, 26
  in quantum physics, 25

R
Rapport-connection, 131–132
Recovery strategies
  goals of, 116
  for resourceful state recovery, 116
Refocusing and neuroplasticity, 37
Reframing, 37
  and neuroplasticity, 37
  semantic memory, 83–84
Re-imprinting
  definition of, 70
  memory reconsolidation using, 70–71
  semantic memory, 83
Relabeling, 45
  and neuroplasticity, 37
REM sleep, memory formation during, 103–104
Resource in context of problem, 46
Revaluing and neuroplasticity, 38
"Reward circuit"
  and dopamine, 164–165
  hippocampus response, 58
  neurotransmitters in, 157
  for problems
    advantages of, 157
    disadvantages of, 158, 160
Right-brain, 186
  functions of, 183
  inductive language patterns to stimulate, 190
  and left-brain
    structural differences between, 183–184
    switching between, 184–191
  and left-brain, differences between, 186–187
  preferences of, 188
  skills, drawing on client's, 189
Right-brain stroke, 186
Right hemisphere, 181

S
Salivation, 16
Scanning techniques, advances in, 14–15
Self. *See also* Identity
  embodied, 234
  emotional, 231, 234
  experiencing, 232–233, 235

group, 232
mirrored, 232
as nonexistent, 231–232
as object, 231
senses of, 230–231
sensor-of-the-world concept of, 230
spiritual sense of, 231, 232
Self-directed neuroplasticity, 30
Dr. Schwartz's model for, 32, 36
coaching, 38–40
labeling, 40–41
refocusing, 37
reframing, 37
relabeling, 37
revaluing, 38
from traditional Buddhism, 31
Semantic memory, 56
as belief, 82–83
beliefs and values as, 125
Change Personal History patterns, 81–82
changing using submodalities, 85–87
definition of, 82
originated from episodic memories, 80, 82–83
reframing of, 83–84
Sensor-of-the-world concept of self, 230
Sensory experience
of anxiety, 86–87
creating, 86
Sensory information, 170
Serotonin, 156
Sign language, 226
Singing and right-brain activity, 187
Skull, 12
Sleep and learning, 103–104
Space
to anchor resources, 219–221
blended, 218
as context, 216–218
act of climbing Squaw Peak, 217–218
emotional states, 217
exercise, 218–219
memory of, 140
as metaphor, 228
Space and movement, metaphors of
coaching tips for, 203–204
cultures and languages, 205–206

in everyday speech, 202–203
landscape learning, 206–207
London cab drivers, 206–207
"near" and "far" concept. J
and "far" concept
research on, 205–207
Space-time metaphors, 221
and cultural differences, 222
physical movement and
landscape, 222–22(
example, 222–226
language patterns, 226–2:
timeline imagine, 222
Spatial anchors
definition of, 219
for specific states, 222
way to use, 220
Spatial awareness exercises, 140
Spatial language, 204
Spiritual sense of self, 231, 232
Split-brain experiments, 14
Spoken language, brain areas act
213–214
State-dependent learning, 43
State-dependent memory, 28
"Stealing anchors," 20
Stop the world state. See Peripher
Stress response, 65–66, 137, 171
Strokes, 186
Submodalities
auditory and kinesthetic, 85
of client's visual system, 85
definition of, 85, 144
and map-across technique, 1∠
unconscious coding, 145
and visual cortex, 141–144
Swish pattern technique
and information coding, 148-
movement of picture, 148
Symbolic language
areas for processing, 183
Sympathetic nervous system, 39

T
Temporary sensitivity, 24
Temptation, deferred, 43–44
Thoughts
labeling, 40–41

purpose of, 64
Top-down learning, 117
Top-down processing, 42–43
Trance
    and change work, 78–79
    induction, 190

U
Unconscious foreknowledge in decision-
    making, importance of, 247–248
Unconscious minds, 67, 136, 187
    decision making, 245–249
    solution and right-brain, 188–189
Unconscious processing and memory
    formation, 65–66

V
Vision, 141
Visual anchor, 18
Visual cortex, 17, 141, 145
    memories stored in, 145–147
    and moving objects, 142
    visual process. See Visual process
    working of, 148
Visualization training, 48
Visual process, 142
    brain role in, 143
    and V1, 142
    What pathway, 143
    Where pathway, 143

Visual processing, 141
Visual reality, 143–144
Visual squash, 195
    balancing left-brain and right-brain
        activities, 196
    performing, 197–201
V-K dissociation pattern
    client example of, 175–179
    submodality shifts, 174
Von Economo cells, 237

W
Wada test, 194–195
Wernicke's area, 14, 183
Word search puzzles, 121
Working memory, 80, 148, 251
    areas of, 56–57
    definition of, 56
    experiencing own, 59
    formation of, 88–89
    and learning circuit. See Learning
        circuit
    limitations and problems of, 63
    metaphor for thinking about, 57
    paying attention to, 95–96
    and reward circuit. See "Reward
        circuit"
    timing importance in, 57
    usage in coaching, 59–62
    visual and auditory loops of, 57

Made in the USA
Las Vegas, NV
28 November 2022

60592899R00146